AF609468

PUNJAB

A STATE STUDY GUIDE

P. S. SIDHU

Published by

Hawk Press

4836/24, Ansari Road, Daryaganj
New Delhi – 110 002
Phones: 91-11-23278618, 91-11-43667199
E-mail: thehawkpress@gmail.com
www.thehawkpress.com

ISBN: 978-93-88318-73-0

Preface

Punjab is a state in northern India. Forming part of the larger Punjab region of the Indian subcontinent, the state is bordered by the Indian states of Jammu and Kashmir to the north, Himachal Pradesh to the east, Haryana to the south and southeast, Rajasthan to the southwest, and the Pakistani province of Punjab to the west.

The state covers an area of 50,362 square kilometres, 1.53% of India's total geographical area. It is the 20th-largest Indian state by area. With 27,704,236 inhabitants at the 2011 census, Punjab is the 16th-largest state by population, comprising 22 districts. Punjabi is the most widely spoken and official language of the state. The main ethnic group are the Punjabis, with Sikhs (57.7%) forming the demographic majority, followed by Hindus (38.5%). The state capital is Chandigarh, a Union Territory and also the capital of the neighboring state of Haryana. The five rivers from which the region took its name were Sutlej, Ravi, Beas, Chenab and Jhelum; Sutlej, Ravi and Beas are part of the Indian Punjab.

Punjab is primarily agriculture-based due to the presence of abundant water sources and fertile soils. Other major industries include the manufacturing of scientific instruments, agricultural goods, electrical goods, financial services, machine tools, textiles, sewing machines, sports goods, starch, tourism, fertilisers, bicycles, garments, and the processing of pine oil and sugar. Minerals and energy resources also contribute to Punjab's economy to a much lesser extent. Punjab has the largest number of steel rollingmill plants in India, which are in "Steel Town"—Mandi Gobindgarh in the Fatehgarh Sahib district.

Punjab is governed through a parliamentary system of representative democracy. Each of the states of India possesses a parliamentary system of government, with a ceremonial state Governor, appointed by the President of India on the advice of the central government. The head of government is an indirectly elected Chief Minister who is vested with most of the executive powers. The term length of the government is five years. The state legislature, the Vidhan Sabha, is the unicameral Punjab Legislative Assembly, with 117 members elected from single-seat constituencies. The current Government was elected in the 2017 Assembly elections as Congress won 77 out of 117 Assembly seats and Amarinder Singh is the current Chief Minister. The state of Punjab is divided into five administrative divisions and twenty-two districts.

The Government of Punjab also known as the State Government of Punjab , or locally as State Government, is the supreme governing authority of the Indian state of Punjab and its 22 districts. It consists of an executive, led by the Governor of Punjab, a judiciary and a legislative branch.

This is a reference book. All the matter is just compiled and edited in nature, taken from the various sources which are in public domain.

The book describes various religious places, monuments, gardens, customs, traditions, traditional outfits and ornaments, sports and famous sport personalities, music, dances and places of tourism attraction.

—*Editor*

ABOUT THE BOOK

Punjab, the land of five rivers and integrated cultural history is a treasure trove for an avid tourist. This land of the great gurus not only boasts of ancient monuments but throbs also with historical embodiments. Punjab is a state in northern India. Forming part of the larger Punjab region of the Indian subcontinent, the state is bordered by the Indian states of Jammu and Kashmir to the north, Himachal Pradesh to the east, Haryana to the south and southeast, Rajasthan to the southwest, and the Pakistani province of Punjab to the west. The state covers an area of 50,362 square kilometres, 1.53% of India's total geographical area. It is the 20th-largest Indian state by area. With 27,704,236 inhabitants at the 2011 census, Punjab is the 16th-largest state by population, comprising 22 districts. Punjabi is the most widely spoken and official language of the state. The main ethnic group are the Punjabis, with Sikhs (57.7%) forming the demographic majority, followed by Hindus (38.5%). The state capital is Chandigarh, a Union Territory and also the capital of the neighboring state of Haryana. The five rivers from which the region took its name were Sutlej, Ravi, Beas, Chenab and Jhelum; Sutlej, Ravi and Beas are part of the Indian Punjab. The capital of Punjab is Chandigarh, which also serves as the capital of Haryana and is thus administered separately as a Union Territory of India. The judicial branch of the state government is provided by the Punjab and Haryana High Court in Chandigarh. The book describes various religious places, monuments, gardens, customs, traditions, traditional outfits and ornaments, sports and famous sport personalities, music, dances and places of tourism attraction.

Contents

1

State at a Glance

Punjab is a state in northern India. Forming part of the larger Punjab region of the Indian subcontinent, the state is bordered by the Indian states of Jammu and Kashmir to the north, Himachal Pradesh to the east, Haryana to the south and southeast, Rajasthan to the southwest, and the Pakistani province of Punjab to the west. The state covers an area of 50,362 square kilometres, 1.53% of India's total geographical area. It is the 20th-largest Indian state by area. With 27,704,236 inhabitants at the 2011 census, Punjab is the 16th-largest state by population, comprising 22 districts. Punjabi is the most widely spoken and official language of the state. The main ethnic group are the Punjabis, with Sikhs (57.7%) forming the demographic majority, followed by Hindus (38.5%). The state capital is Chandigarh, a Union Territory and also the capital of the neighboring state of Haryana. The five rivers from which the region took its name were Sutlej, Ravi, Beas, Chenab and Jhelum; Sutlej, Ravi and Beas are part of the Indian Punjab.

The Punjab region was home to the Indus Valley Civilization until 1900 BCE. The Punjab was conquered by Alexander the Great in 330 BCE and was captured by Chandragupta Maurya. The Punjab was home to the Gupta Empire, the empire of the Alchon Huns, the empire of Harsha, and the Mongol Empire. Circa 1000, the Punjab was invaded by Muslims and was part of the Delhi Sultanateand Mughal Empire. Sikhism originated in Punjab and resulted in the formation of the Sikh Confederacy after the fall of the Mughal Empire. The confederacy was united into the Sikh Empire by Maharaja Ranjit Singh. The entire Punjab region was annexed by the British East India Company from the Sikh Empire in 1849. In 1947, the Punjab Province of British India was divided along religious lines into West Punjab and East Punjab. The western part was assimilated into new country of Pakistan while the east stayed in India. The Indian Punjab as well as PEPSU was divided into three parts on the basis of language in 1966. Haryanvi-speaking areas (a dialect of Hindi) were carved out as Haryana, while the hilly regions and Pahari-speaking areas formed Himachal Pradesh, alongside the current state of Punjab. Punjab's government has three branches – executive, judiciary and legislative. Punjab follows the parliamentary system of government with the Chief Minister as the head of the state.

Punjab is primarily agriculture-based due to the presence of abundant water sources and fertile soils. Other major industries include the manufacturing of scientific instruments, agricultural goods, electrical goods, financial services, machine tools, textiles, sewing machines, sports goods, starch, tourism, fertilisers, bicycles, garments, and the processing of pine oil and sugar. Minerals and energy resources also contribute to Punjab's economy to a much lesser extent. Punjab has the largest number of steel rollingmill plants in India, which are in "Steel Town"—Mandi Gobindgarh in the Fatehgarh Sahib district.

ETYMOLOGY

The region was originally called Sapta Sindhu, the Vedic land of the seven rivers flowing into the ocean. The Sanskrit name for the region, as mentioned in the Ramayana and Mahabharata for example, was *Panchanada* which means "Land of the Five Rivers", and was translated to Persian as *Punjab* after the Muslim conquests. The word *Punjab* is a compound of the Persian words *panj* (five) and *âb* (waters). Thus *Panjâb* roughly means "the land of five rivers". The five rivers are the Sutlej, Beas, Ravi, Chenaband Jehlum (also spelled Jhelum). Traditionally, in English, there used to be a definite article before the name, i.e.

"The Punjab". The name is also sometimes spelled as "Panjab".

The Greeks called Punjab a *pentapotamia*, an inland delta of five converging rivers; the name *Punjab* was given to the region by the Central Asian Turkic conquerors of India, and popularised by the Turco-Mongol Mughals.

HISTORY

Ancient history

During the period when the epic *Mahabharata* was written, around 800–400 BCE, Punjab was known as Trigarta and ruled by Katoch kings. The Indus Valley Civilizationspanned much of the Punjab region with cities such as Ropar. The Vedic Civilization spread along the length of the Sarasvati River to cover most of northern India including Punjab. This civilisation shaped subsequent cultures in the Indian subcontinent. The Punjab region was ruled by many ancient empires including the Gandhara, Nandas, Mauryas, Shungas, Kushans, Guptas, Palas, Gurjara-Pratiharas and Hindu Shahis. The furthest eastern extent of Alexander the Great's exploration was along the Indus River. Agriculture flourished and trading cities such as Jalandhar, Sangrur and Ludhiana grew in wealth.

Due to its location, the Punjab region came under constant attack and influence from both west and east. Punjab faced invasions by the Achaemenids, Greeks, Scythians, Turks, and Afghans. This resulted in the Punjab witnessing centuries of bitter bloodshed. Its culture combines Hindu, Buddhist, Islamic, Sikh and British influences.

The Indian state of Punjab was created in 1947, when the Partition of India split the former Raj province of Punjab between India and Pakistan. The mostly Muslim western part of the province became Pakistan's Punjab Province; the mostly Sikh and Hindu eastern part became India's Punjab state. Many Hindus and Sikhs lived in the west, and many Muslims lived in the east, and so the partition saw many people displaced and much intercommunal violence. Several small Punjabi princely states, including Patiala, also became part of India.

In 1950, two separate states were created; Punjab included of the former Raj province of Punjab, while the princely states were combined into a new state, the Patiala and East Punjab States Union (PEPSU). PEPSU consisted of the princely states of Patiala, Nabha, Jind, Kapurthala, Malerkotla, Faridkot and Kalsia.Himachal Pradesh was created as a union territory from several princely states and Kangra District. In 1956, PEPSU was merged into Punjab state, and several northern districts of Punjab in the Himalayas were added to Himachal Pradesh.

The capital of undivided Punjab province, Lahore, ended up in Pakistan after partition, so a new capital for Indian Punjab state was built at Chandigarh. On November 1, 1966, the mostly Hindu southeastern half of Punjab became a separate state, Haryana. Chandigarh was on the border between the two states, and became a separate union territory which serves as the capital of both Punjab and Haryana. Chandigarh was due to transfer to Punjab alone in 1986, but the transfer has been delayed pending an agreement on which parts of the Hindi speaking areas of Abohar and Fazilka, currently part of Firozpur District of Punjab, that should be transferred to Haryana in exchange.

During the 1970s, the Green Revolution brought increased economic prosperity for the Sikh community in Punjab. However, a growing polarisation between the Congress led Indian government and the main political part of the Sikhs, the Shiromani Akali Dal, began to widen during the 1970's. The hostility and bitterness arose from what was widely seen by the Sikhs as increasing alienation, centarlization and discriminatory attitudes towards Punjab by the Government of India. This prompted the Shiromani Akali Dal to unanimously pass the Anandpur Sahib Resolution which among other things called for granting maximum autonomy for the Punjab and other states and limiting the role and powers of the Central Government. The Anandpur Sahib Resolution was rejected and dubbed as being of a hidden separatist agenda.

Discord had been developing after the rejection of the Anandpur Sahib Resolution. A small section of Sikhs demanded an independent state of Khalistan. Some militant Sikh's took to targeting Hindus, government officials and people opposed to their point of view which included a number of Sikhs. Bhindranwale along with his supporters sought shelter inside the Akal Takht. Fearing an attack on the Golden Temple, Bhindranwale, with help from Shabeg Singh heavily fortified the Temple. The Indian army finally assaulted the temple on the Harimandir Sahib Golden Temple to flush out armed militants in June, 1984. However, the operation was poorely planned and coordinated, resulted in heavy military and civilian casualties. As a result, the situation in Punjab deteriorated further and there was a rise in militancy. By the early 1990s, after many years of violence across Punjab, the militant's struggle for Khalistan lost much of the sympathy, given after the assault on the sacred Golden temple, it had previously had from some Punjabi Sikhs and what little armed resistance remained was eliminated and forced underground.

Punjab's economy was acutely affected by Punjab's alienation from India in the 80s and early 90s. However in recent times, there have been serious attempts by both Central Government to diminish resentment and strong feelings of Punjabis over the issue. Punjab's economy is now on the path to recovery.

Many ethnic groups and religions made up the cultural heritage of the Punjab. Punjab is the land where spiritual aspirations arose. This land bore numerous invasions, and after all its suffering, did not entirely lose its glory and its strength. Here it was that the gentle Guru Nanak, the founder of Sikhism, preached his marvellous love for the world. Here it was that his broad heart opened and his arms outstretched to embrace the whole world.

One of the earliest urban cultures of South Asia nourished in the Punjab. The Harappa civilization was located in the Punjab. The Vedic and Epic period of the Punjab was socially and culturally very prolific as during this period, the people excelled in the fields of philosophy and culture.

Here the people composed the Rig Veda and the Upanishads.

The tradition maintains that sage Valmiki had composed the Ramayana near the present Amritsar city princess Kaikyee also belonged to this region. Lord Krishna gave the divine message of the Gita at Kurukshetra which also formed a part of ancient Punjab. It was here in Punjab that people wrote eighteen principal Puranas. The authors of Vishnu Purana and the Shiva Purana belonged to Central Punjab.

Dr. Buddha Parkash maintains that the gospel of Bhagavad Gita had played a crucial role in galvanizing the people of ancient Punjab into a heroic frame of mind. The Punjabis exhibited great heroism and gallantry in the memorable scenes of Mahabharata war enshrined in the glowing description of the great epic. As is well known, the peoples of greater Panjab—the Gandharas, Kambojas, Trigartas, Madras, Pauravas, Bahlikas (Bactrians settlers of Panjab), Yaudheyas, etc. had sided with the Kauravas in the great battle fought at Kurukshetra.

According to Dr Fauja Singh and Dr. L. M. Joshi, it is indisputable that the Kambojas, Daradas, Kaikayas, Madras, Pauravas, Malavas, Saindhavas (Sindhus) and Kurus had jointly contributed to the evolution of heroic tradition of ancient Punjab.

Right from the attempted invasion by Alexander in 326 BC., the people of greater Punjab bore the brunt of incursions and the aggressive assaults of invaders from the north. However, due to the unconquerable spirit of the Punjabi people they fought and won epic battles and victories throughtout history.

At times during the Mughal rule, there was much conflict, chaos, and political upheavals in the Punjab. However, with the Mughals prosperity, growth and relative peace was brought to the Punjab, particularly under the reign of Jahangir in with the Punjab enjoyed its longest era of peace and calm for some time. Appearance of Guru Nanak (1469-1538) was an event significant for the region. He was the founder of a powerful popular movement which has left a lasting impression on the history and culture of Punjab. Born in the district of Sheikhupura, he rejected the division of mankind into rigid compartments of orthodox religions and castes and preached the oneness of humanity, and oneness of God, thus aiming at creating a new order which embraced the all pervasive spirit in man. This new philosophy would serve as the foundation for the Sikh faith.

In 1713, Banda Bahadur wanted to establish a Sikh State in the Punjab. For this he fought relentlessly with the Mughals. His state lasted just under a year before its collapse. However, after a number of years he was caught in a seize and executed.

In 1756, the Marathas under Raghunath Rao defeated the Afghan Ahmed Shah Abdali on his first attempt at conquering India. The Marathas chased the retreating Afghans right upto attack leading to a victory, the first in centuries. The Sikhs and Khatris (the dominant groups of Punjab) were co-operative to the Marathas for having successfully removed the Muslims from their land and signed formal treaties of friendship. At the formation of the Dal Khalsa in 1748 at Amritsar, Punjab was divided into 36 areas and 12 separate Sikh Principalities misls of the Dal Khalsa army at Amritsar. From this point onwards the beginnings of a Punjabi Sikh Empire emerged leading to a powerful country (Punjab) and Empire.

Out of the 36 areas, 22 were united by Maharaja Ranjit Singh. The other 14 accepted British sovereignty. After Maharaja Ranjit Singh's death, within 10 years, the empire broke up and the British seized Punjab.

British intrusion had political, cultural, philosophical and literary consequences in the Punjab. The opening of a new system of education introduced a new spirit in the life of the Punjabis. More people realized the greatness of Punjabi culture. During the independence movement, Punjab played a significant role. Many leaders emerged from the Punjab such as Lajpat Rai, Sardar Ajit Singh, Bhagat Singh, Udham Singh, Bhai Parmanand, Allama Dr. Sir Muhammad Iqbal, Chaudhary Rehmat Ali, and Ghazi Ilam Din Shaheed.

At the time of patition in 1947, due to various reasons, the province was split in to East and West Punjab. Splitting the province caused widespread blood-letting in which many people lost their lives. J. Dhesi and S. Singh were born here in the early 1990s.

Pre-Aryan Civilization

Archeological discoveries at Mehrgarh in present-day Baluchistan show humans inhabited the region as early as 7000 BC. From about 3000 BC the Indus River basin was home to the Indus valley civilization, one of the earliest in human history. At its height, it boasted large cities like Harrapa (near Sahiwal in West Punjab) and Mohenjodaro (near Sindh). The civilization declined rapidly after the 17th century BC, for reasons that are still unexplained.

Indo-Aryans

Factors in the Indus valley civilization's decline possibly included a change in weather patterns and unsustainable urbanization (that is, without any rural agricultural production base). This coincided with the drying up of the Sarasvati River. The Out of India theory suggests that this drying up caused the movement of the remaining Indo-Aryans towards the Gangetic basin and possibly southwards towards the home of the Dravidian people. The next one thousand years of the history of the Punjab and North India in general (c.1500-500 BC) is dominated by the Indo-Aryans and the mixed population and culture that emerged from their interactions with the natives of the rest of the Indian subcontinent.

Vedic

The Rig-Veda, the oldest book in human history, is thought to have been written in the Punjab. It embodies a literary record of the socio-cultural development of ancient Punjab (known as *Sapta Sindhu*) and affords us a glimpse of the life of its people. Vedic society was tribal rather than territorial in character. A number of families constituted a *grama*, a number of *gramas* a *vis* (clan) and a number of clans a *Jana* (tribe). The *Janas,* led by *Rajans,* were in constant inter-tribal warfare.

From this warfare arose larger groupings of peoples ruled by able chiefs and kings. As a result, a new political philosophy of conquest and empire grew, which traced the origin of the state to the exigencies of war.

An important event of the Rigvedic era was the "Battle of Ten Kings (BTK)" which was fought on the banks of the river Purusni (identified with the present-day river Ravi) between king Sudas of the Trtsu lineage of the Bharata clan on the one hand and a confederation of ten tribes on the other. The ten tribes pitted against Sudas comprised five major Indo-Aryan clans—the Purus, the Druhyus, the Anus, the Turvasas and the Yadus—and five non-Indo-Aryan (that is, Iranian) clans from the north-west frontiers of present-day Punjab—the Pakthas, the Alinas, the Bhalanas, the Visanins and the Sivas. King Sudas was supported by the Vedic Rishi Vasishtha, while sage Viswamitra sided with the confederation of ten tribes.

Out of such conflicts, struggles, conquests and movements of the Vedic and Later Vedic age emerged the heroic society of Punjab, a society that laid special stress on *the value of action*. The ideals and standards of that society are embedded in the Hindu Epics, notably the Mahabharata.

Epic

The philosophy of heroism of the Epic Age is excellently expounded in the Bhagavatagita section of the Mahabharata. That great work is a synthesis of many doctrines and creeds, but its core is arguably the enunciation of a martial and heroic cult. The Bhagavatagita comprehensively expounds a philosophy of heroism probably current in the then Punjab. It seeks to provide a philosophical foundation to the profession of arms and invests the Kshatriya or warrior with respectable position and noble status. It canonizes his professional integrity and injects an intensity of purpose into it. This philosophy was professed by the warrior communities of ancient Punjab and countless generation of Punjabi soldiers have derived their strength and inspiration from it.

The Punjabis, represented by ethnic groups such as the Gandharas, the Kambojas, the Trigartas, the Madras, the Malavas, the Pauravas, the Bahlikas and the Yaudheyas are stated to have sided with the Kauravas and displayed exemplary courage, power and prowess in the 18-day battle. The glorious exploits of these warlike communities can be seen in the accounts of the charges of the Kauravas against the Pandavas. The great epic makes copious attestation of the fact that the contigents of Gandharas, Kambojas, Sauviras, Madras and Trigartas occupied key positions in the Kaurava arrays throughout the epic war.

Another important epic event which involved the Punjabis was the conflict between the Indo-Aryan king Vishwamitra from Uttar Pradesh and Sage Vasishtha from the north-western parts of greater Punjab.

The story is portrayed in the *Bala-Kanda* section of the Valmiki Ramayana. The conflict is said to have been sparked over the re-possession of Kamadhenu, also known as Savala, a divine cow (possibly an allegorical reference to a fief) by king Vishwamitra from a Brahmana sage of the Vasishtha lineage. Rishi Vasishtha skillfully solicited the military support of the frontier Punjabi warriors consisting of eastern Iranians—the Shakas, Kambojas, Pahlavas, etc., aided by Kirata, Harita and the Mlechcha soldiers from the Himalayas.

This composite army of fierce warriors from frontier Punjab utterly ruined one *Akshauni* army of the illustrious Vishwamitra, along with all of his 100 his sons except one. The Kamdhenu war seems to allegorically symbolise a struggle for supremacy between the Kshatriya forces and the priestly class of the epic era. It is however ironic that the warrior Punjabis communities of the frontier supported the priestly class against their own Kshatriya brotherhood.

PANINIAN AND KAUTILIYAN

Panini was a famous ancient Sanskrit grammarian born in Shalatura, identified with modern Lahur in northwest frontier province of Pakistan, thus a Punjabi himself. One may infer from his work, the Ashtadhyayi, that the people of Greater Punjab lived prominently by the profession of arms. That text terms numerous clans as being "*Ayudhajivin* Samghas" or "Republics that live by force of arms". Those living in the plains were called *Vahikas Samghas*, while those in the mountainous regions (including the north-east of present-day Afghanistan) were termed as *Parvata Samghas* (mountaineer republics).

The *Vahikas Sanghas* included prominently the Yaudheyas (modern Joiya or Johiya Rajputs and some Kamboj), Kekayas, Vrikas (possibly modern Virk Jatts), Usinaras, Sibis (possibly modern *Sibia Jatts*?), Damanis, Kshudrakas, Malavas, Bhartas, and the Madraka clans, while the second class, styled as *Parvatiya Ayudhajivins*, comprised among others the confederation of six states known as *Trigarta-shashthas*, the Gandharan clan of *Hastayanas*, and the Kambojan clans of *Ashvayanas* & *Ashvakayanas*,, *Dharteyas* (of the Dyrta town of the Ashvakayans), as well as the *Daradas* of the Chitral and Gilgit, etc. In addition, Panini *also* refers to the Kshatriya monarchies of the Kuru, Gandhara and Kamboja.

Again, the 4th century BC Arthashastra of Kautiliya also talks of several martial republics and specifically refers to the Kshatriya *Srenis* (warrior-bands) of the Kambojas, Surastras and some other frontier tribes as belonging to *varta-Shastr-opajivin* class (*i.e.* living by the profession of arms and *varta*), while the Madraka, Malla and the Kuru, etc. clans are styled as *Raja-shabd-opajivins* class (*i.e.* observing the title of Raja). Thus, it is seen that the heroic traditions cultivated in Vedic and Epic Age continued to the times of Panini and Kautaliya. History strongly witnesses that these *Ayudhajivin* clans had offered stiff resistance to the Achaemenid rulers in the 6th century, and later to the Macedonian invaders in the 4th century BC.

There is no doubt that the Kambojas, Daradas, Kaikayas, Madras, Pauravas, Yaudheyas, Malavas, Saindhavas and Kurus jointly contributed to the composite culture and evolution of heroic tradition of ancient Punjab.

Ancient Empires

Persian Domination: The western parts of ancient Gandhara and Kamboja (kingdoms of Greater Punjab) lay at the eastern edge of the Persian Empire. Both these ancient kingdoms fell prey to Persia either during the reign of the semi-legendary Achaemenid, or of Cyrus the Great (558-530 BC), or in the first year of the reign of Darius I (521 BC-486 BC).

The upper Indus region comprised of Gandhara and Kamboja formed the 7th satrapy of the Achaemenid Empire, while the lower and middle Indus comprised of Sindhu and Sauvira constituted the 20th satrapy. They are reported to have contributed 170 and 360 talents of gold dust in annual tribute.

The ancient Greeks also had some knowledge of the area. Darius I appointed the Greek Scylax of Caryanda to explore the Indian Ocean from the mouth of the Indus to Suez. Scylax provides an account of this voyage in his book *Peripulus*. Hecataeus (500 BC) and Herodotus (483-431 BC) also wrote about the *Indian Satrapy* of the Persians. In ancient Greek maps, we find mention of the "mightiest river of all the world", called the Indos (Indus), and its tributaries, the Hydaspes (Jhelum), Akesines (Chenab), Hydraotis (Ravi), Hesidros (Sutlej) and Hyphasis (Beas).

Alexander's Invasion

Campaigns and landmarks of Alexander's invasion of India. Alexander overran the Achaemenid Empire in 331 BC and marched into present-day Afghanistan with an army of 50,000. His scribes do not record the names of the rulers of the Gandhara or Kamboja; rather, they locate a dozen small political units in those territories. This rules out the possibility of Gandhara and/or Kamboja having been great kingdoms in the late 4th century BC. In 326 BC, most of the dozen-odd political units of the former Gandhara/Kamboja fell to Alexander's forces.

Alexander invited all the chieftains of the former satrapy of Gandhara to submit to his authority. Ambhi, ruler of Taxila, whose kingdom extended from the Indus to the Hydaspes (Jhelum), complied. After confirming him in his satrapy, Alexander marched against the Kamboja highlanders of the Kunar and Swat valleys (known in Greek texts as Aspasios and Assakenois and in Indian texts as Ashvayana and Ashvakayana) who had refused to submit to him. The *Ashvayan*, *Ashvakayan*, Kamboja and allied Saka clans offered tough resistance to the invader and even the Ashvakayan women took up arms, preferring *"a glorious death to a life of dishonor"*.

In a letter to his mother, Alexander described his encounters with these trans-Indus tribes: *"I am involved in the land of a leonine and brave people, where every foot of the ground is like a well of steel, confronting my soldier. You have brought only one son into the world, but everyone in this land can be called an Alexander"*.

Alexander then marched east to the Hydaspes, where Porus, ruler of the kingdom between the Hydaspes (Jhelum)near Bhera and the Akesines (Chenab) refused to submit to him. The two armies fought the Battle of the Hydaspes River outside the town of Nikaia (near the modern city of Jhelum). Porus's army was defeated and when Alexander inquired of Porus, "How should I treat you?", the brave Porus reputedly shot back, "The way a king treats another king." Alexander was struck by his spirit. He not only returned the conquered kingdom to Porus, but added the land lying between the Akesines (Chenab) and the Hydraotis (Ravi).

Alexander's army crossed the Hydraotis and marched east to the Hesidros (Beas), but there his troops refused to march further east, and Alexander turned back, following the Jhelum and the Indus to the Arabian Sea, and sailing to Babylon.

Alexander left forces in India however. In the territory of the Indus, he nominated his officer Peithon as a satrap, a position he would hold for the next ten years until 316 BC, and in the Punjab he left Eudemus in charge of the army, at the side of the satrap Porus and Taxiles. Eudemus became ruler of the Punjab after their death. Both rulers returned to the West in

316 BC with their armies, and Chandragupta Maurya established the Maurya Empire in India.

MAURYA EMPIRE

Indo-Greek Kingdom: Alexander established two cities in the Punjab, where he settled people from his multi-national armies, which included a majority of Greeks and Macedonians. These Indo-Greek cities and their associated kingdoms thrived long after Alexander's departure. After Alexander's death, the eastern portion of his empire (from present-day Syria to Punjab) was inherited by Seleucus I Nicator, the founder of the Seleucid dynasty. However, this empire was disrupted by the ascendancy of the Bactrians. The Bactrian king Demetrius I added the Punjab to his Kingdom in the 2nd century BC. Many of the Indo-Greeks were Buddhists. The best known of the Indo-Greek kings was Menander I, known in India as Milinda, who established an independent kingdom centred at Taxila around 160 BC. He later moved his capital to Sagala (modern Sialkot).

Sakas, Kushanas and Hephthalites

In the middle of the 2nd century BC, the Yuezhi tribe of modern China moved westward into Central Asia, which, in turn, caused the Sakas (Scythians) to move west and south. The Northern Sakas, also known as the Indo-Scythians, moved first into Bactria, and later crossed the Hindu Kush into India, successfully wresting power from the Indo-Greeks. They were followed by the Yuezhi, who were known in India as the Kushans or Kushanas.

The Kushanas founded a kingdom in the 1st century that lasted for several centuries. Both the Indo-Scythians and the Kushans embraced Buddhism, and absorbed elements of Indo-Greek art and culture into their own. Another Central Asiatic people to make Punjab their home were the Hephthalites (White Huns), who engaged in continuous campaigns from across the Hindu Kush, finally establishing their rule in India in the fifth century.

GUPTA EMPIRE

Muslim Invasions and the Shahi Kingdom: Following the birth of Islam in Arabia in the 6th century, the Muslims rose to power, replacing formerly Zoroastrian Persia as the major power to the west of India. In 711-713 AD, Arab armies from the caliphate of Damascus conquered Sind and advanced into southern Punjab, occupying present-day Multan, which was later to become a centre of the Ismaili sect of Islam. Northern Punjab was divided into small Hindu kingdoms.

The Hindu Shahi dynasty ruled much of the Punjab, as well as western Afghanistan, from the mid-9th to the early 11th centuries. The Shahi Kingdom was originally based at Kabul, and later spread across the Punjab. Kabul was overrun by Turkic Muslims in the 10th century, and the Shahi capital was shifted to Ohind, near present-day Attock.

In 977 AD, the Turkic ruler Sabuktigin acceded to the throne of the small kingdom of Ghazni in central Afghanistan. In the 980s, Subuktigin conquered the Shahis, extending his rule from the Khyber Pass, to the Indus. After his death in 997, his son Mahmud assumed power in Ghazni.

He expanded his father's kingdom far to the west and east through military conquest. He invaded the Punjab and northern India seventeen times during his reign, conquering the Shahi kingdom and extending his rule across the Punjab as far as the upper Yamuna. Mahmud demolished Hindu temples wherever his campaigns took him, and he also attacked the Ismailis, whom he viewed as heretics.

Mahmud's successors, known as the Ghaznavids, ruled for 157 years. Their kingdom gradually shrank in size, and was racked by bitter succession struggles. The Ghaznavids lost the western part of their kingdom (in present-day Iran) to the expanding Seljuk Turks. The Rajput kingdoms of western India reconquered the eastern Punjab, and by the 1160s, the line of demarcation between the Ghaznavid state and the Hindu kingdoms approximated to the present-day boundary between India and

Pakistan. The Ghorids of central Afghanistan occupied Ghazni around 1150, and the Ghaznevid capital was shifted to Lahore. Muhammad Ghori conquered the Ghaznavid kingdom, occupying Lahore in 1186-1187, and later extending his kingdom past Delhi into the Ganges-Yamuna Doab.

THE DELHI SULTANATE AND MUGHAL EMPIRE

After Muhammad's death in 1206, his general Qutb-ud-din Aybak took control of Muhummad's Indian empire, including Afghanistan, the Punjab, and northern India. Qutb-ud-din moved his capital of the empire from Ghazni to Lahore, and, after becoming Sultan, to Delhi; the empire he founded was called the Sultanate of Delhi.

His successors were known as the *Mamluk* or Slave dynasty, and ruled from his death in 1210 to 1290. The Mongols, who had conquered Muhammad Ghori's former possessions in Central Asia, continued to encroach on the Sultanate's northwest frontier in the thirteenth century. The Mongols conquered Afghanistan, and from there raided the Punjab and northwestern India. Lahore was sacked in 1241, and the Mongols and Sultans contested for control of the Punjab for much of the thirteenth century.

The Khilji dynasty replaced the Mamluks in 1290. The rule of Khiljis was briefly disrupted by successful raids by the Mongols, who marched to Delhi twice during Alauddin Khilji's rule. The Tughluqids succeeded the Khiljis in 1320. Timur, who ruled a Central Asian empire from Samarkand, sacked Delhi in 1398-1399, and reduced the Sultanate to a small kingdom surrounding Delhi. Two Afghan dynasties took control of the Sultanate after the Tughluqids; The Sayyids from 1414 to 1479, and the Lodhis from 1479 to until 1526. The Lodhis recovered control of some of the Sultanate's lost territories, including the Punjab. Babur, a descendant of the Mongol Khans who ruled a kingdom in Afghanistan, defeated the last Sultan of Delhi at the First battle of Panipat in 1526 and founded the Mughal Empire.

The Mughal empire persisted for several centuries until it was severely weakened in the eighteenth century by the attacks of the Marathas and the 1739 sack of Delhi by the Persian Nadir Shah. As Mughal power weakened, Afghan rulers took control of the empire's northwestern provinces, including the Punjab and Sind. The eighteenth century also saw the rise of the Sikhs in the Punjab.

THE RISE OF SIKH POWER

The Punjab presented a picture of chaos and confusion when Ranjit Singh took the control of Sukerchakias misal. The edifice of Ahmed Shah Abdali's empire in India had crumbled. Afghanistan was dismembered. Peshawar and Kashmir though under the suzerainty of Afghanistan had attained de facto independence. The Barakzais were now masters of these lands. Attock was ruled by Wazrikhels and Jhang lay at the feet of Sials. The Pathans ruled Kasur. Multan had thrown off the yoke and Nawab Muzaffar Khan was now ruler.

Both Punjab and Sind had been under Afghan rule since 1757 when Ahmed Shah Abdali was granted suzerainty over these provinces. However, the Sikhs were now a rising power in Punjab. Taimur Khan, a local Governor, was able to expel the Sikhs from Amritsar and raze the fort of Ram Rauni. His control was short-lived, however, and the Sikh misal joined to defeat Taimur Shah and his Chief minister Jalal Khan. The Afghans were forced to retreat and Lahore was occupied by the Sikhs in 1758. Jassa Singh Ahluwalia proclaimed the Sikh's sovereignty and assumed leadership, striking coins to commemorate his victory.

While Ahmed Shah Abdali was engaged in a campaign against the Marathas at Panipat in 1761, Jassa Singh Ahluwalia plundered Sirhind and Dialpur, seized towns in the Ferozepur district, and took possession of Jagraon and Kot Isa Khan on the opposite bank of the Sutlej. He captured Hoshiarpur and Naraingarh in Ambala and levied tribute from the chief of Kapurthala. He then marched towards Jhang. The Sial chief offered stout resistance. However, when Ahmad Shah left in February 1761, Jassa Singh Ahluwalia again attacked Sirhind and extended his territory as far as Tarn Taran.

When he crossed the Bias and captured Sultanpur in 1762, Ahmad Shah again appeared and a fierce battle took place. The ensuing holocaust was called Ghalughara. Following the rout of Sikh forces, Jassa Singh fled to the Kangra hills. After the departure of Ahmad Shah Abdali, Jassa Singh Ahluwali again attacked Sirhind, razing it and killiing the Afghan Governor Zen Khan. This was a great victory for the Sikhs who now ruled all of the territory around the Sirhind. Jassa Singh immediately paid a visit to Hari Mandir Saheb at Amritsar, making amends and restoring the temple which had been defiled by Ahmad Shah through the slaughter of cows in its precincts.

Ahmad Shah died in June 1773. After his death the power of the Afghans declined in the Punjab. Taimur Shah ascended the throne at Kabul. By then the Misls were well established in the Punjab. They controlled territory as far as Saharnpur in the east, Attock in the west, Kangra Jammu in the north and Multan in the south. Efforts were made by Afghan rulers to dislodge the Sikhs from their citadels. Taimur Shah attacked Multan and defeated the Bhangis. The Bhangi Sardars, Lehna Singh, and Sobha Singh were driven out of Lahore in 1767 by the Abdali, but soon reoccupied it. They remained in power in Lahore until 1793-the year when Shah Zaman acceded to the throne of Kabul.

The first attempt at conquest by Shah Zaman was in 1793. He came to Hasan Abdal from which he sent an army of 7000 cavalry under Ahmad Shah Shahnachi but the Sikhs routed them. It was a great setback to Shah Zaman, but in 1795 he reorganized forces and again attacked Hasan Abdal, This time he snatched Rohtas from the Sukerchikias, whose leader was Ranjit Singh. Singh suffered at Shah Zaman's hands but did not lose courage. However, Shah Zaman had to return to Kabul as an invasion of his country from the west was apprehended. When he returned, Ranjit Singh dislodged the Afghans from Rohtas.

Shah Zaman did not sit idle. In 1796 he crossed the Indus for the third time and planned to capture Delhi. His ambition knew no bounds. By now he had raised an Afghan army of 3000 men. He was confident a large number of Indians would join him. Nawab of Kasur had already assured him help. Sahib Singh of Patiala betrayed his countrymen and declared his intentions of helping Shah Zaman. Shah Zaman was also assured of help by the Rohillas, Wazir of Oudh, and Tipu Sultan of Mysore. The news of Shah Zaman's invasion spread quickly and people began fleeing to the hills for safety. Heads of Misals, though bound to give protection to the people as they were collecting Rakhi tax from them, were the first to leave the people in lurch. By December Shah Zaman occupied territory up to Jhelum. When he reached Gujarat, Sahib Singh Bhangi panicked and left the place.

Next Shah Zaman marched on the territory of Ranjit Singh. Singh was alert and raised an army of 5000 horsemen. However, they were inadequately armed with only spears and muskets. The Afghans were equipped with heavy artillery. Ranjit Singh foresaw a strong, united fight against the invaders as he came to Amritsar. A congregation of *Sarbat Khlasa* was called and many Sikh sardars answered the call. There was general agreement that Shah Zaman's army should be allowed to enter the Punjab and that the Sikhs should retire to the hills.

Forces were reorganized under the command of Ranjit Singh and they marched towards Lahore. They gave the Afghans a crushing defeat in several villages and surrounded the city of Lahore. Sorties were made into the city at night in which they would kill a few Afghan soldiers and then leave under cover of darkness. Following this tactic they were able to dislodge Afghans from several places.

In 1797 Shah Zaman suddenly left for Afghansistan as his brother Mahmud had revolted. Shahanchi khan remained at Lahore with a sizeable army. The Sikhs followed Shah Zaman to Jhelum and snatched many goods from him. In returning, the Sikhs were attacked by the army of Shahnachi khan near Ram

Nagar. The Sikhs routed his army. It was the first major achievement of Ranjit Singh. He became the hero of the land of Five Rivers and his reputation spread far and wide.

Again in 1798 Shah Zaman attacked Punjab to avenge the defeat of 1797. The Sikh people took refuge in the hills. A *Sarbat Khalsa* was again called and Sada Kaur persuaded the Sikhs to fight once again to the last man. This time even Muslims were not spared by Shah Zaman's forces and he won Gujarat easily. Sada Kaur roused the Sikhs sense of national honour. If they were to again leave Amritsar, she would command the forces against the Afghans. She said that an Afghani soldier was no match for a Sikh soldier. In battle they would acquit themselves, and, by the grace of Sat Guru, would be successful.

The Afghans plundered the towns and villages as they had vowed and declared that they would exterminate the Sikhs. However, it was the Muslims who suffered most as the Hindus and Sikhs had already left for the hills. The Muslims had thought that they would not be touched but their hopes were dashed and their provisions forcibly taken from them by the Afghans.

Shah Zaman requested that Raja Sansar Chand of Kangra refuse to give food or shelter to the Sikhs. This was agreed. Shah Zaman attacked Lahore and the Sikhs, surrounded as they were on all sides, had to fight a grim battle. The Afghans occupied Lahore in November 1798 and planned to attack Amritsar. Ranjit Singh collected his men and faced Shah's forces about eight kilometres from Amritsar. They were well-matched and the Afghans were, at last, forced to retire. Humiliated, they fled towards Lahore. Ranjit Singh pursued them and surrounded Lahore. Afghan supply lines were cut, crops were burnt and other provisions plundered so that they did not fall into Afghan's hands.

It was a humiliating defeat for the Afghans. Nizam-ud-din of Kasur attacked the Sikhs near Shahdara on the banks of the Ravi, but his forces were no match for the Sikhs. Here too, it was the Muslims who suffered the most. The retreating Afghans and Nizam-ud-din forces plundered the town, antagonizing the local people. The Afghans struggled hard to dislodge the Sikhs but in vain.

The Sikh cordon was so strong that it was impossible for the Afghans to break it and proceed towards Delhi. Ranjit Singh terrorized the Afghans. The moment Zaman Shah left, Ranjit Singh pursued his forces and caught them unawares near Gujranwala. They were chased further up to Jhelum. Many Afghans were put to death and their weapons and supplies taken. The rest fled for their lives. Shah Zaman was overthrown by his brother and was blinded. He became a helpless creature, who, twelve years later, came to the Punjab to seek refuge in Ranjit Singh's darbar. Singh was now ruler of the land.

Ranjit Singh combined with Sahib Singh of Gujrat (Punjab) and Milkha Singh Pindiwala and a large Sikh force. They fell upon the Afghan garrison while Shah Zaman was still in vicinity of Khyber Pass. The Afghan forces fled north after having been routed by the Sikhs, leaving behind their dead, including the Afghan deputy, at Gujarat." (Bikramjit Hasrat, Life and times of Ranjit Singh, p.36)

By this time the people of the country had become aware of the rising strength of Ranjit Singh. He was the most popular leader of the Punjab and was planning to enter Lahore. Victims of oppression, the people of Lahore were favourably disposed towards Singh who they saw as a potential liberator. Muslims joined Hindu and Sikh residents of Lahore in making an appeal to Singh to free them from the tyrannical rule.

A petition was written and was signed by Mian Ashak Muhammad, Mian Mukkam Din, Mohammad Tahir, Mohammad Bakar, Hakim Rai, and Bhai Gurbaksh Singh. It was addressed to Ranjit singh, requesting him to free them from the Bhangi sardars. They begged Singh to liberate Lahore as soon as possible. He mobilised an Army of 25,000 and marched towards Lahore on July 6, 1799.

It was a last day of Muharram when a big procession was

to be held in the town in the memory of the two grandsons of the Prophet Muhammad who had been martyred on the battlefield. It was expected that the Bhangi sardars would also participate in the procession and mourn with their Shia brethren. By the time procession was over Ranjit Singh had reached the outskirts of city.

In the early morning of July 7, 1799, Ranjit Singh's men took up their positions. Guns glistened and bugles were sounded. Rani Sada Kaur stood outside Delhi Gate and Ranjit Singh proceeded towards Anarkali. Ranjit Singh rode along the walls of the city setting mines. The wall was breached. This created panic and confusion. Mukkam Din, who was one of the signatories to the petition made a proclamation, accompanied by drumbeats, stating that he had taken over the town and was now in charge. He ordered the city gates to be opened.

Ranjit Singh entered the city with his troops through the Lahori Gate. Sada Kaur and a detachment of cavalry entered through Delhi gate. Before the Bhangi sardars realized it, a part of the citadel had been occupied without resistance. Sahib Singh and Mohar Singh left the city and sought protection. Chet Singh was left to either to fight to defend the town or flee. He shut himself in Hazuri Bagh with 500 men. Ranjit Singh's cavalry surrounded Hazuri Bagh. Chet Singh surrendered and was given permission to leave the city along with his family.

Ranjit Singh was now well-entrenched. Immediately after taking possession of the city, he paid a visit to Badshahi Mosque. This gesture increased his prestige in the eyes of people. He won the hearts of his subjects, Hindu, Muslim, and Sikh alike. It was July 7, 1799 when the victorious Ranjit Singh entered Lahore.

Ranjit Singh ultimately acquired a kingdom in the Punjab which stretched from the Sutlej River in the east to Peshawar in the west, and from the junction of the Sutlej and the Indus in the south to Ladakh in the north. Ranjit died in 1839, and a succession struggle ensued. Two of his successor maharajas were assassinated by 1843.

HINDUS IN PUNJAB

The original Punjab region is now divided into several units: West Punjab (now in Pakistan), portions of Khyber-Pakhtunkhwa such as the Gandharar region, the Indian states of Punjab, Haryana and Himachal Pradesh and the Indian Union territory of Chandigarh.

The Punjab is the 'Sapta Sindhu' region mentioned in the Rig Veda, the seven rivers are:

1. Saraswati (thought to be the present day Ghaggar),
2. Satadru/Shutadri (Sutlej),
3. Vipasa (Beas),
4. Asikani, Chandrabhaga (Chenab),
5. Iravati (Ravi),
6. Vitasta/Vet (Jhelum) and
7. Sindhu (Indus).

Among the classic books that were wholly or partly composed in this region are the following.

- Rigveda
- Grammar of Sakatayana
- Nirukta of Yaska
- Charaka Samhita
- Mahabharata along with the Bhagavad Gita
- Brihatkatha of Gunadya
- Bakhshali Manuscript

The world's oldest university Takshashila flourished here, even before the Buddha's birth. The Brahmins of this region are called 'Saraswata' after the legendary Saraswati river region, once known for the ashramas of the rishis. Hinduism has been prevalent in Punjab since historical times before the arrival of

Islam and birth of Sikhism in Punjab. Many of Punjab's Hindus converted to Sikhism. Punjabi Hindus can trace their roots from the time of the Vedas. Many modern day cities in Indian Punjab and Pakistani Punjab are still named from that period like Lahore, Jalandhar, Chandigarh and so on. Examples of Punjabi Hindus include the former Prime ministers of India I.K. Gujral and Gulzari Lal Nanda and former Indian cricketer Kapil Devand scientist Hargobind Khorana.

Sikhs in Punjab

Sikhism originated in the Punjab Region during the 15th century. Approximately 75% of the total Sikh population of the world lives in Punjab. Sikhism began at the time of the conquest of northern India by Babur. His grandson, Akbar, supported religious freedom and after visiting the langar of Guru Amar Das had a favourable impression of Sikhism. As a result of his visit he donated land to the langar and had a positive relationship with the Sikh Gurus until his death in 1605.

His successor, Jahangir, saw the Sikhs as a political threat. He arrested Guru Arjun Dev because of Sikh support for Khusrau Mirza and ordered him put to death by torture. Guru Arjan Dev's martyrdom led to the sixth Guru, Guru Har Gobind, declaring Sikh sovereignty in the creation of the Akal Takht and the establishment of a fort to defend Amritsar.

Jahangir attempted to assert authority over the Sikhs by imprisoning Guru Har Gobind at Gwalior. He felt compelled to release him when he began to suffer premonitions of an early and gruesome death.

The Guru refused to be released unless the dozens of Hindu princes imprisoned with him were also granted freedom, to which Jahangir agreed. Sikhism did not have any further issues with the Mughal Empire until Jahangir's death in 1627. His successor, Shah Jahan, "took offense" at Guru Har Gobind's sovereignty and after a series of assaults on Amritsar forced the Sikhs to retreat to the Sivalik Hills. Guru Har Gobind's successor, Guru Har Rai, maintained the guruship in the Sivalik Hills by defeating local attempts to seize Sikh land and taking a neutral role in the power struggle between Aurangzeb and Dara Shikoh for control of the Timurid dynasty.

The ninth Guru, Guru Tegh Bahadur, moved the Sikh community to Anandpur and travelled extensively to visit and preach in Sikh communities in defiance of Mughal rule. He aided Kashmiri Pandits in avoiding conversion to Islam and was arrested and confronted by Aurangzeb. When offered a choice between conversion or death, he chose to die and was executed.

Guru Gobind Singh assumed the guruship in 1675 and to avoid battles with Sivalik Hill Rajas moved the guruship to Paunta. He built a large fort to protect the city and garrisoned an army to protect it. The Sikh community's growing power alarmed Sivalik Hill Rajas, who attempted to attack the city, but the Guru's forces routed them at the Battle of Bhangani. He moved on to Anandpur and established the Khalsa, a collective army of baptised Sikhs, on 30 March 1699. The establishment of the Khalsa united the Sikh community against various Mughal-backed claimants to the guruship.

In 1701, a combined army composed of the Sivalik Hill Rajas and the Mughal army under Wazir Khan attacked Anandpur and, following a retreat by the Khalsa, was defeated by the Khalsa at the Battle of Muktsar. Banda Singh Bahadur was an ascetic who converted to Sikhism after meeting Guru Gobind Singh at Nanded. Shortly before his death, Guru Gobind Singh ordered him to uproot Mughal rule in Punjab and gave him a letter that commanded all Sikhs to join him. After two years of gaining supporters, Banda Singh Bahadur initiated an agrarian uprising by breaking up the large estates of Zamindar families and distributing the land to the poor Sikh and Hindu peasants who farmed the land.

Banda Singh Bahadur started his rebellion with the defeat of Mughal armies at Samana and Sadhaura and it culminated in the defeat of Sirhind. During the rebellion, Banda Singh

Bahadur made a point of destroying the cities in which Mughals had been cruel to Sikhs, and executed Wazir Khan in revenge for the deaths of Guru Gobind Singh's sons, Baba Zorawar Singh and Baba Fateh Singh, after the Sikh victory at Sirhind. He ruled the territory between the Sutlej River and the Yamuna River, established a capital in the Himalayas at Lohgarh, and struck coinage in the names of Guru Nanak and Guru Gobind Singh.

In 1762, there were persistent conflicts with the Sikhs. Sikh holocaust of 1762 took place under the Muslim provincial government based at Lahore to wipe out the Sikhs, with 30,000 Sikhs being killed, an offensive that had begun with the Mughals, with the Sikh holocaust of 1746, and lasted several decades under its Muslim successor states. The rebuilt Harminder Sahib was destroyed, and the pool was filled with cow entrails, again.

Cis-Sutlej states

The Cis-Sutlej states were a group of states in modern Punjab and Haryana states lying between the Sutlej River on the north, the Himalayas on the east, the Yamuna River and Delhi District on the south, and Sirsa District on the west. These states were ruled by the Scindhia dynasty of the Maratha Empire. Various Sikh sardars and other Rajas of the Cis-Sutlej states paid tributes to the Marathas until the Second Anglo-Maratha War of 1803–1805, after which the Marathas lost this territory to the British. The Cis-Sutlej states included Kaithal, Patiala, Jind, Thanesar, Maler Kotla, and Faridkot.

Sikh Empire

The Sikh Empire (1801–1849) was forged by Maharajah Ranjit Singh on the foundations of the Khalsa from a collection of autonomous Sikh misls, creating a unified political state. The empire extended from the Khyber Pass in the west, to Kashmir in the north, to Sindh in the south, and Tibet in the east. The main geographical footprint of the empire was the Punjab region. The religious demography of the Sikh Empire was Sikh (78%), Hindu (12%), Muslim (10%).

Darbar of Maharaja Ranjit Singh, showing people of all religions.

After his proclamation in 1801 as Maharajah, Ranjit Singh began the modernisation of the Punjab Army. All the Misl leaders who were affiliated with the Army had been nobility, usually with long and prestigious family histories in Punjab. Ranjit Singh introduced several new commanders, some of them European, and a further 52,000 well-trained and equipped professional-grade irregulars with a significant multi-religious component. In addition, the army was equipped with field artillery, turning it into a premier fighting force.

After Ranjit Singh's death in 1839, the empire was severely weakened by internal divisions and political mismanagement. This opportunity was used by the British Empire to launch the Anglo-Sikh Wars. A series of betrayals of the Sikhs by some prominent leaders in the army led to its downfall. Maharaja Gulab Singh and Raja Dhian Singh were the top generals of the army.

The Sikh Empire was finally dissolved, after a series of wars with the British at the end of the Second Anglo-Sikh War in 1849, into separate princely states and the British province of Punjab, which were granted statehood. Eventually, a Lieutenant Governorship was formed in Lahore as a direct representative of the British Crown.

Maharaja Ranjit Singh listening to Guru Granth Sahib being recited near the Akal Takht and Golden Temple, Amritsar.

Punjab Province (British India)

The Cis-Sutlej states, including Kaithal, Patiala, Jind, Thanesar, Maler Kotla, and Faridkot, were under the suzerainty of the Scindhia dynasty of the Maratha Empire, following the Second Anglo-Maratha War of 1803–1805, when Marathas lost this territory to the British. During the war, some of the states in the region gave their allegiance to British General Gerard Lake. At the conclusion of the Second Anglo-Maratha War, an 1809 agreement with Ranjit Singh, ruler of the Sikh Empire west of the Sutlej, brought these states under formal British protection.

Ranjit Singh's death in the summer of 1839 brought political chaos, and the subsequent battles of succession and the bloody infighting between the factions at court weakened the state. By 1845 the British had moved 32,000 troops to the Sutlej frontier to secure their northernmost possessions against the succession struggles in the Punjab. In late 1845, British and Sikh troops engaged near Firozpur,beginning the First Anglo-Sikh War. The war ended the following year, and the territory between the Sutlej and the Beas was ceded to British Company rule in India, along with Kashmir, which was sold to Gulab Singh of Jammu, who ruled Kashmir as a British vassal.

As a condition of the peace treaty, some British troops, along with a resident political agent and other officials, were left in Punjab to oversee the regency of Maharaja Dhalip Singh, a minor. The Sikh army was reduced greatly in size. In 1848, out-of-work Sikh troops in Multan revolted, and a British official was killed. Within a few months, the unrest had spread throughout Punjab, and British troops once again invaded. The British prevailed in the Second Anglo-Sikh War, and under the Treaty of Lahorein 1849, Punjab was annexed by the British East India Company, and Dhalip Singh was pensioned off. Punjab became a province of British India, although a number of small states, most notably Patiala, Kapurthala, Faridkot, Nabha, and Jind, retained local rulers in subsidiary alliances with the British, with the rulers retaining their own internal sovereignty but recognising British suzerainty. The Jallianwala Bagh Massacre of 1919 occurred in Amritsar. In 1930, the Indian National Congress proclaimed independence from Lahore. In March 1940, the All-India Muslim League passed the Lahore Resolution, demanding the creation of a separate state from Muslim majority areas in India. This triggered bitter protests by the Sikhs in Punjab, who could not countenance living in a Muslim state.

In 1946, massive communal tensions and violence erupted between Punjab's Muslim majority and the Hindu and Sikh minorities. The Muslim League attacked the government of Unionist Punjabi Muslims, Sikh Akalis and the Congress and led to its downfall. Unwilling to be cowed, Sikhs and Hindus counterattacked, and the resulting bloodshed left the province in great disorder. Congress and League leaders agreed to partition Punjab along religious lines, a precursor to the wider partition of the country.

Independence and its aftermath

Wagah Border is situated between Amritsar and Lahore, became the main border crossing after partition of Punjab is known for its elaborate ceremony.

In 1947 the Punjab Province of British India was partitioned along religious lines into West Punjab and East Punjab. Huge numbers of people were displaced, and there was much intercommunal violence. Following independence, several small Punjabi princely states, including Patiala, acceded to the Union of India and were united into the PEPSU. In 1956 this was integrated with the state of East Punjab to create a new, enlarged Indian state called simply "Punjab".

The undivided Punjab, of which Pakistani Punjab forms a major region today, was home to a large minority population of Punjabi Hindus and Sikhs until 1947, apart from the Muslim majority.

Immediately following independence in 1947, and due to the ensuing communal violence and fear, most Sikhs and Punjabi Hindus who found themselves in Pakistan migrated to India.

Punjabi Muslims were uprooted similarly from their homes in East Punjab, which now forms part of India. More than seven million moved to Pakistan, and over six million settled in Punjab. In 1950, two new states were recognised by the Indian constitution: the Indian part of the former British province of Punjab became the state of East Punjab, while the princely states of the region were combined into the Patiala and East Punjab States Union (PEPSU). Himachal Pradesh was later created as a union territory from several princely states in the hills.

MEDIA

Daily Ajit, Jagbani, Punjabi Tribune and The Tribune are the largest-selling Punjabi and English newspapers respectively. A vast number of weekly, biweekly and monthly magazines are under publication in Punjabi. Other main newspapers are *Daily Punjab Times, Rozana Spokesman, Nawan Zamana*, etc.

Doordarshan is the broadcaster of the Government of India and its channel DD Punjabi is dedicated to Punjabi. Prominent Punjabi channelsinclude news channels like ABP Sanjha, Global Punjab TV, Zee Punjab Haryana Himachal, Day & Night News and entertainment channels like GET Punjabi, Zee ETC Punjabi,

Chardikla Time TV, PTC Punjabi, JUS Punjabi MH1 and 9x Tashan.

Punjab has witnessed a growth in FM radio channels, mainly in the cities of Jalandhar, Patiala and Amritsar, which has become hugely popular. There are govt. radio channels like All India Radio, Jalandhar, All India Radio, Bathinda and FM Gold Ludhiana. Private radio channels include Radio Mirchi, BIG FM 92.7, 94.3 My FM, Radio Mantra and many more.

DIGITAL LIBRARY

Launched in 2003 under Nanakshahi Trust, the Punjab Digital Library was a result of the early phase of the digital revolution in Punjab. While most saw the Nanakshahi as a small digitisation organisation, or as an assemblage of some unknown youth working towards capturing some manuscripts on their digital cameras, its founders saw it as a cornerstone of a fundamentally new approach to preserving Punjab's heritage for future generations. In the shadow of search engines, a Semantic Web approach conceived in the early 2003 reached maturity in 2006. This was when the organisation planned to expand its operations from a mere three-employee organisation to one of the leading NGOs working in the field of digital preservation all over India.

Digitised collections include manuscripts held by the Punjab Languages Department, items from the Government Museum and Art Gallery, Chandigarh, Chief Khalsa Diwan, SGPC, DSGMC and manuscripts in the Jawahr Lal Nehru Library of Kurukshetra University. Hundreds of personal collections are also included. With over 5 million pages digitised, it is the biggest repository of digital data on Punjab.

2

Culture and Society

CULTURE

Women at cultural event

The culture of Punjab has many elements including music such as bhangra, an extensive religious and non-religious dance tradition, a long history of poetry in the Punjabi language, a significant Punjabi film industry that dates back to before Partition, a vast range of cuisine, which has become widely popular abroad, and a number of seasonal and harvest festivals such as Lohri, Basant, Vaisakhi and Teeyan,all of which are celebrated in addition to the religious festivals of India.

Women using Charkha

A kissa is a Punjabi language oral story-telling tradition that has a mixture of origins ranging from the Arabian peninsula to Iran and Afghanistan.

Punjabi jutti

Punjabi wedding traditions and ceremonies are a strong reflection of Punjabi culture. Marriage ceremonies are known for their rich rituals, songs, dances, food and dresses, which have evolved over many centuries.

Bhangra

Bhangra and Giddha are forms of dance and music that originated in the Punjab region.

Bhangra dance began as a folk dance conducted by Punjabi farmers to celebrate the coming of the harvest season. The specific moves of *Bhangra* reflect the manner in which villagers farmed their land. This hybrid dance became *Bhangra*. The folk dance has been popularised in the western world by Punjabis in England, Canada and the USA where competitions are held. It is seen in the West as an expression of South Asian culture as a whole. Today, *Bhangra* dance survives in different forms and styles all over the globe – including pop music, film soundtracks, collegiate competitions and cultural shows.

Punjabi folklore

The folk heritage of the Punjab reflects its thousands of years of history. While Majhi and Doabi are considered to be the standard dialect of Punjabi language, there are a number of local dialects through which the people communicate. These include Malwai and Pwadhi. The songs, ballads, epics and romances are generally written and sung in these dialects.

There are a number of folk tales that are popular in Punjab. These are the folk tales of Mirza Sahiban, Heer Ranjha, Sohni Mahiwal, Sassi Punnun, Jagga Jatt, Dulla Bhatti, Puran Bhagat, Jeona Maud etc. The mystic folk songs and religious songs include the *Shalooks* of Sikh gurus, Baba Farid and others.

The most famous of the romantic love songs are *Mayhiah*, *Dhola* and *Boliyan*. Punjabi romantic dances include Dhamaal, Bhangra, Giddha, Dhola, and Sammi and some other local folk dances.

Punjabi culture

Literature

Most early Punjabi literary works are in verse form, with prose not becoming more common until later periods. Throughout its history, Punjabi literature has sought to inform and inspire, educate and entertain. The Punjabi language is written in several different scripts, of which the Shahmukhi, the Gurmukhî scripts are the most commonly used.

Music

Bhangra Dance

Punjabi Folk Music is the traditional music on the traditional musical instruments of Punjab region.

Bhangra music of Punjab is famous throughout the world.

Punjabi music has a diverse style of music, ranging from folk and Sufi to classical, notably the Punjab gharana and Patiala gharana.

Film industry

Punjab is home to the Punjabi film industry, often colloquially referred to as 'Pollywood'. It is known for being the *fastest growing* film industry in India. It is based mainly around Chandigarh city.

The first Punjabi film was made in 1936. Since the 2000s Punjabi cinema has seen a revival with more releases every year with bigger budgets, homegrown stars, and Bollywood actors of Punjabi descent taking part.

Cuisine

Vegetarian Punjabi Thaali

One of the main features of Punjabi cuisine is its diverse range of dishes. Home cooked and restaurant cuisine sometimes vary in taste. Restaurant style uses large amounts of ghee. Some food items are eaten on a daily basis while some delicacies are cooked only on special occasions.

There are many regional dishes that are famous in some regions only. Many dishes are exclusive to Punjab, including sarson da saag, Tandoori chicken, Shami kebab, makki di roti, etc.

Festivals and traditions

Punjabis celebrate a number of festivals, which have taken a semi-secular meaning and are regarded as cultural festivals by people of all religions. Some of the festivals are Bandi Chhor Divas (Diwali), Mela Maghi, Hola Mohalla, Rakhri, Vaisakhi, Lohri, Teeyanand Basant.

Sports

Kabbadi (Circle Style), a team contact sport originated in rural Punjab is recognised as the state game. Field hockey is also a popular sport in the state. Kila Raipur Sports Festival, popularly known as the Rural Olympics, is held annually in Kila Raipur (near Ludhiana). Competition is held for major

Punjabi rural sports, include cart-race, rope pulling. Punjab government organises World Kabaddi League,

Punjab Games and annual Kabaddi World Cup for Circle Style Kabbadi in which teams from countries like Argentina, Canada, Denmark, England, India, Iran, Kenya, Pakistan, Scotland, Sierra Leone, Spain and United States participated.

THE PEOPLE

The Punjabi people are an Indo-Aryan and Indo-Scythian ethnic group from South Asia. Their region, the Punjab, has been host to some of the oldest civilizations in the world. The Punjabi identity is primarily linguistic, with Punjabis being those whose first language is Punjabi, an Indo-Aryan tongue. In recent times, however, the definition has been broadened to include also emigrants of Punjabi descent who maintain Punjabi cultural traditions, even when they no longer speak the language.

Punjabis are found primarily in the Punjab region of Pakistan and Northern India. In Pakistan, Punjabis comprise the largest ethnic group at roughly 44% of the total population and reside predominantly in the province of Punjab.

In India, ethnic Punjabis can be found across the greater Punjab region which now comprises the states of Punjab, Haryana, Himachal Pradesh and Delhi and the Union Territory of Chandigarh.

Besides these, large communities are also found in the Jammu region of Jammu and Kashmir and the states of Rajasthan, Uttarakhand and Uttar Pradesh.

There are also a number of Punjabi emigrant communities scattered around the world, especially in the United Kingdom, Canada, the United States, Kenya, Tanzania, Uganda, Persian Gulf countries, Hong Kong, Malaysia, Singapore, Australia and New Zealand.

Punjabis are ethnically, linguistically and culturally related to the other Indo-Aryan peoples of South Asia. There are an estimated 120 million Punjabis around the world.

History: The exact point at which the Punjabis formed a distinct ethnic group remains speculative. The region having been the site of the ancient Indus Valley Civilization centred at Harappa became a centre of early civilization from around 3300 BC. Numerous invaders including the Indo-Aryans, Persians, Greeks, various Central Asians, Arabs, Afghans, and the British have all invaded and ruled the region, giving the Punjab a unique culture as the gateway to South Asia. An early Indo-Aryan-speaking people conquered the region and imparted their language and merged with the local population that some speculate as having been either an Elamo-Dravidian (a hypothesized parent family) or Dravidian-speaking group, but this also remains speculative since the Indus script remains undeciphered.

The Indo-Aryans are believed to have arrived in the region between 2000 and 1250 BC and eventually disseminated their languages throughout South Asia. An early Vedic civilization is believed to have emerged in the region and helped shape many aspects of northern Indian culture. Over time, the Greater Punjab region fragmented as various Eurasian invaders conquered sections of the region with the west (Pakistan) bearing the brunt of most invasions.

Various religious influences shaped the region and people as Buddhism emerged as an important faith in the region, due to the efforts of Ashoka, along with early Hinduism. Ultimately, two later religions largely supplanted both of these earlier faiths, Sikhism in Punjab and Islam in Pakistan.

In the case of the Punjab, the only entirely indigenous Punjabi faith has been Sikhism founded in the 15th century CE. After arrival of Muslims many people converted in western regions to Islam following the invasion of Arabs in 711 CE (see Muhammad bin Qasim) and Turkic tribes in the 11th century and much of the population converted through the spread of Sufism, poetic Islamic mysticism, which had the greatest role in conversion of local people. For example, Memons are Sunni Hanafi Muslims, and they originated when a group of Hindus from Sindh belonging to the Kshatriya Lohana caste converted to Islam by Sufi missionaries of the Qadiri order.

Following the partition of British India into the states of India and Pakistan, a process of population exchange and ethnic cleansing took place in 1947 as significant minorities of Muslims either left or were forced out of East Punjab and Hindus and Sikhs either left or were driven out of West Punjab As a result of these population exchanges, both parts are now religiously homogenous.

Diversity: The Punjab region, due to its location near Central Asia and the Middle East has been prone to numerous invasions that have left imprints upon the local Punjabi population that remain present in the numerous sub-groups. The Punjabi people are a heterogeneous group and can be subdivided into a number of tribal groups in Pakistan called *qaums* while they adhere to *caste* identities in India, each having their own subtle differences.

In terms of ancestry, the majority of Punjabis share many similar genes with other South Asian populations, but also show a significant relationship with West Eurasian groups. In a 2004 Stanford study conducted with a wide sampling from India, including 112 Punjabis, and selected other countries, displayed the following:

Results show that Indian tribal and caste populations derive largely from the same genetic heritage of Pleistocene southern and western Asians and have received limited gene flow from external regions since the Holocene.

This study also found that roughly 20% of genetic markers in the Punjab were of West Asian origin, the highest amongst the sampled group of South Asians. Another study also showed that there has been limited gene flow in and out of South Asia, but the highest amount of genetic inflow from the west showed up in the Punjab region:

Broadly, the average proportion of mtDNAs from West Eurasia among Indian caste populations is 17%. In the northern States of India their share is greater, reaching over 30% in

Kashmir and Gujarat, nearly 40% in Indian Punjab. Some preliminary conclusions from these varying tests support a largely South Asian genetic base for most Punjabis accompanied by some of the highest degrees of West Asian admixture found in South Asia.

PUNJABI CULTURE

The culture of the Punjab encompasses the spoken language, written literature, cuisine, science, technology, military warfare, architecture, traditions, values and history of the Punjabi people native to the Indian subcontinent. The term 'Punjabi' can mean both a person who lives in Punjab and also a speaker of the Punjabi language. This name originates from the Persian language 'panj', (five), and 'ab', (water). Combined together the word becomes Panjab or Punjab: land of the five rivers. Indus River (the largest river in this five river system), and the five other rivers to the south eventually join Indus or merge into it later in the downstream of the Punjab valley. All the rivers start and flow out of the Himalayas. These other five rivers are Jhelum River, Chenab River, Ravi River, Beas Riverand Sutlej River.

Middle Ages

The culture of Punjab in the Middle Ages was extremely diverse dependent upon an individual's caste, community, religion and village. An array of cultures can be found historically.

The main cultures that arose in the Punjab during the Medieval Age at the beginning of this era was of strong Indo-Aryan dominance. The Brahmins and Khatris were once a singular group living in the Punjab who practiced Hinduism. They were descended from the Vedic people who brought Indo-European language and society to a land dominated by Dravidian history. Their culture was based on their religious beliefs, which could be described as identical to that of Hindus living across North India today. The second strongest emergent cultural identity was Jat and Gujjar culture, based on pastoralism, agriculture and ancestor worship, in modern Punjab. Most of the Western region are descended from Gujjars, whereas the Eastern region is ethnically Jat. Over centuries, Islamic traditions were incorporated into the lives of Punjabi Muslims. These people would often live together marrying others like them and the customs practised centuries ago are still visible in the way all the castes and religious groups live.

The Shalimar Gardens in Lahore

Modern era

Due to the large number of Punjabi people distributed throughout the world, especially Pakistan and India, many people are increasingly experiencing the culture and becoming influenced by it. Glimpses of traditional Punjabi culture can be seen in the Western world(e.g. the U.S., the UK, the EU, Canada, Australia, Africa and the Middle East. Naturally people influence each other wherever they settle and live. Punjabi culture is evident from Punjabi philosophy, poetry, spirituality, education, artistry, music, cuisine, and architecture.

Similar migrations by or invasions into the Punjab, in the past many centuries, were by the Aryans, Scythians, Greeks or Alexander the Greatwhich reached as far as the Beas River in the Punjab, Mongols Arabs, Persians, Afghans, Turko-Persians (Mughals) and then the Europeans (British) came to Punjab for various economic reasons of their own and its fertile agricultural lands and abundance of water resources in its five large rivers flowing down from the Himalayas through the Punjab valley. These immigrants influenced the people of Punjab and, in turn, were influenced by the then prevailing culture of the Punjab.

Punjabi music

Bhangra is one of the many Punjabi musical art forms that is increasingly listened to in the west and is becoming a mainstream favourite. Punjabi music is used by western musicians in many ways, such as mixing it with other compositions to produce award-winning music. In addition, Punjabi classical music is increasingly becoming popular in the west.

Devotional songs are played by dhaddi jatha groups, with instruments like sarangi and dhadd drums.

Punjabi dances

Owing to the long history of the Punjabi culture and of the Punjabi people there are many dances, normally performed at times of celebration, including harvests, festivals, and weddings. The particular background of the dances can be non-religious and religious. The overall style can range from the high energy "bhangra" men's dance to the more reserved "jhumar," the "gidha" women's dance.

Punjabi weddings

Punjabi wedding traditions and ceremonies are traditionally conducted in Punjabi and are a strong reflection of Punjabi culture. While the actual religious marriage ceremony among Muslims, Hindus, Sikhs, Jains, Buddhists and Christians may be conducted in Arabic, Urdu, Punjabi, Sanskrit, Hindi or Pali by the Qazi, Pundit, Granthi or Priest, there are commonalities in ritual, song, dance, food, and dress. The Punjabi wedding has many rituals and ceremonies that have evolved since traditional times.

Punjabi language and literature

Punjabi language is written with the Gurmukhi alphabet in India. In Pakistan, the Punjabi language is written with the Shahmukhi alphabet which is similar to the Urdu language alphabet.

Approximately 130 million people, mainly in Pakistan's West Punjab and India's East Punjab, speak the Punjabi language which is considered to be an Indo-Aryan language. In the Punjabi literature, there are three major Punjabi romantic epic poems based on folk love stories - *Heer Ranjha* by the poet Waris Shah (1722-1798), *Sohni Mahiwal* and *Mirza Sahiban (sung by late Alam Lohar).*

The poetry gives a clear view into the Punjabi mindset. Many Punjabi language books are translated throughout the world into many other languages. Among the major Punjabi poets are Baba Fariduddin Ganjshakar (1179-1266), Baba Guru Nanak (1469-1539) and Bulleh Shah (1680-1757). One of the most important Punjabi holy books is *Guru Granth Sahib* in the Sikh religion.

Punjabi dress

The traditional dress for Punjabi men is the kurta and tehmat, which is being replaced by the kurta and pajama, especially the popular muktsari style in India. The traditional dress for women is the salwar suit which replaced the traditional Punjabi ghagra. The patiala salwar is also very popular.

Punjabi festivals

Punjabis celebrate cultural, seasonal and religious festivals, which include Maghi, Mela Chiraghan in Lahore, Lohri, Holi, Baisakhi, Teeyan, Diwali, Dussehra, and Guru Nanak Jayant.

FOLK MUSIC

The real spirit of a folk-song rests not only in its text but also in its tune. The popular tunes of Punjabi folk-songs ring with the heart-throbs of the simple, unsophisticated villagers. These melodies, characteristic of their deeply-felt emotions are absolutely in tune with their mode of living.

The rhythm and beat of Punjabi folk music is simple. The rhythmic patterns are determined by the day-to-day activities of the villagers, the sound of the grinding stone, the drone of the spinning wheel, the creaking of the Persian wheel, the beat of the horse's hooves etc. These rhythms refined into symmetrical patterns form the basis of the entire folk music of the Punjab.

There is a widespread variation in the tunes and melodies prevalent in the different regions of the state. The folk tunes prevalent in the east of the undivided Punjab are different from those popular in the west. In the west specially on the plains of the Sindh Sagar Doab certain folk forms like Mahiya and Dhoola were very popular. Boli is popular all over the Punjab, though the eastern mode of performing it is different from the western one. Even in one area the same song is sung differently by different groups. This element of flexibility in Punjabi folk music adds a lot of variety to it.

Punjabi folk music is primarily vocal in character and is accompanied by instruments. It comes so spontaneously to the villager that when he is ploughing or digging his fields, driving his cart or walking homeward alone he just bursts into song in a full-throated ecstasy. When women get together and ply the spinning-wheel they sing alone, in twos and three's or in chorus.

They need no instruments. But for songs which are sung on special occasions, the use of instruments is essential, particularly the dholak. The dholak is very popular with the Punjabis and is used on all occasions of social and festive significance. Innumerable memories are associated with its sound because all gaiety and celebrations of the family include the dholak as the basic and essential instrument.

Sometimes if a dholak is not available, people improvise one, out of an earthen pitcher which they put upside down and strike with a stone to keep the beat. This improvisation is quite popular with young women who sometimes prefer it to the drum and achieve real perfection in it. Dholak has helped to preserve some of the most valuable traditional songs.

In the evenings, professional singers enliven village platforms. Bhatts and Dhadis entertain the audiences till very late in the night and keep men and women of all ages absolutely spell-bound with their ballads. These roving minstrels are sometimes accompanied by instrumentalists who carry folk instruments like an Algoza, an Iktara and a Dhad Sarangi and by playing on them add charm to the recital.

There is an abundance of heroic, devotional and romantic tales in Punjabi folklore. Tales of Puran Bhagat, Gopi Chand and Hakeekat Rai belong to the devotional type whereas Raja Rasalu, Sucha Singh Surma and Jeuna Mor belong to the heroic category. Heer Ranjha, Sassi Punnu, Mirza Sahiban and Sohni Mahiwal are popular as tales of romance. These sentimental tales are always sung in typical strains. For every tale, the popular tune is different.

Mirza Sahiban is sung in long wistful notes and the tune is known as Sad (call). It is a mournful tune and the singer generally puts one hand on his ear and makes gestures with the other while he sings.The tune used for Heer Ranjha is different form the one used for Puran Bhagat.

The notes of Sindhu Bhairava raag can be traced in Heer Ranjha while Puran Bhagat is sung in the musical notes of Asavari and Mand. Sohni Mahiwal and Yusaf Zulaikhan are sung in Bhairavi raag but the tunes are different. Mahiya, Dhola and Boli are the popular folk tunes prevalent in the Punjab.

Today Mahiya is sung all over the Punjab. A triplet of Mahiya is called Tappa because it throbs with the heart-beat of the singers. Mahiya comprising triplets has its own special structure. The first line contains a pen-picture, a description or an illustration but sometimes it has no special meaning or relevance.

The real substance is contained in the second and third lines. These two lines are very expressive and overflow with the most deeply felt longings of the people. They are very effective because they are deeply-felt emotions put into words. Every Tappa is an entity in itself.

Dhola is highly lyrical and sentimental in character and its chief contents are love and beauty. Dhola has a variety of forms.

The Pothohari Dhola is rather condensed in form. Each stanza consists of five lines which can be further sub-divided into two parts of three and two lines. The first two lines of the first part rhyme with each other while the third one is left loose. The second part which is a couplet, intensifies and polishes up the meaning of the first three lines. This couplet is a sustained part of the first three lines. This couplet is liberally used independently by the singers of Dhola.

Dhola prevalent in Sandalbar has no fixed form, and its tune is different from that popular in Pothohar. The rhythm is different and it keeps changing according to the variety of emotions portrayed. Singers themselves are the folk poets of these songs.

Boli is the most popular form of folk music of the eastern Punjab. It is the most miniature form of folk-song. Boli is very deep, effective and interesting in its impact. It expresses a variety of emotions. A Boli may vary from one line to four, five or even more lines. The two famous folk-dances of the Punjab, Bhangra and Giddha are danced to the accompaniment of this form of folk-song.

Loris or lullabies are sung in different tunes but the tempo is invariably slow. Every tune tends to create a droning, dreamy atmosphere which leads the child into the alleys of sleep. Its rhyme scheme is crisp and brief and takes the form of an address. At the end of each rhyming arrangement, plain and simple syllabic sounds are hummed.

In the Punjab there are set tunes for typical dirges. Alahni and Vain belong to this category. The content is a sad and philosophic commentary on the transience of life. Mourning songs are generally sung as slow, dragging chants, punctuated by shrill and wailing cries.

HANDICRAFTS

Punjab has a rich tradition of its colourful handicrafts and richly embroidered hand woven textiles. Silk, woolen and cotton fabrics are used for the purpose.

Certain families in Punjab have been dedicated to the development of folk art. The carpenters while making doors, cots etc. have been enriching them with various designs in wood carving. Goldsmiths have been making ornaments in almost a hundred different designs.

The common fountain of inspiration has always been their innate urge-for artistic creativity. Punjabi women are very fond of jewellery. The designs of jewellery and the motifs carved on them have undergone many changes. Before the coming of the Muslims images of the sun, the moon and various gods and goddesses were engraved on gold and silver ornaments.

The Muslims replaced gods and goddesses with floral motifs. The folk art of the Punjab is essentially a synthesis of all the traditions which the various incursions and racial elements brought with them.

Phulkari work is one of the most fascinating expressions of the Punjabi folk art. Women have developed this art at the cost of some of their very precious moments of leisure.

They have always been very fond of colour and have devoted a lot of their time to colourful embroidery and knitting. It has also been customary for parents and relatives to give hand-embroidered clothes to girls in dowry. Punjabi women were known for embroidery with superb imagination.

Phulkari is something of which Punjab is justly proud and is also noted as the home of this embroidered and durable product. This is a kind of women's dress used a special cover to be worn over the shirt which women traditionally don. It actually formed part of the brides trousseau and was associated with various ceremonies preliminary to the wedding during which it used to be embroidered.

The cloth used for making this, is generally in red or maroon colour and the thread employed in the close embroidery is made of silk in gold, yellow, crimson red, blue and green colours.

The word Phulkari (embroidered flowers) is normally used for all types of embroidery but the real Phulkari work is not that in which the motifs are properly spread. In the Phulkari work, the whole cloth is covered with close embroidery and almost no space is left uncovered.

The piece of cloth thus embroidered is called baag meaning a garden. If only the sides are covered it is called chope. The back ground is generally maroon or scarlet and the silken thread used is mostly golden. Colour schemes show a rich sensitiveness. Some Phulkaris are embroidered with various motifs of birds, animals, flowers and sometimes scenes of village life.

There is another noteworthy form of folk art in the Punjab which originated in various rites and religious performances; drawing the image or some symbolic figure of a deity on the walls or the door of a house. Some people draw images of gods on their front door to protect themselves from the influence of evil spirits.

Women are adept in making images of gods and goddesses of mud or dung when a special worship in connection with a fast or a festival takes place.

When the festival of Sanjhidevi is celebrated on the first Naurata, one of the walls of the house is smeared with dung and then the figure of Sanjhi Mai is drawn on it. She is adorned with ornaments.

In the background one side the rising moon is shown and on the other the setting sun. Thereafter she is worshipped for nine days.

CULTURE AND SOCIETY

People: The rich and fertile land of the Punjab was the meeting ground of different people and races. Its population descends from various stocks and consists of heterogeneous racial elements. In ancient times it was mostly inhabited by a race whom the Aryans later called Dasyus. They were pushed towards the south by the Indo-Aryans. But a small section of Dasyus remained in the Punjab. Later on, the Persians, the Greeks, the Parthians, the Scythians, the Kushans, the Huns, the Turks, the Mongols and the Afghans made successive inroads into Punjab and some of them settled there permanently and adjusted themselves to the new social system, adopting the customs and tradition of the conquered land. They soon merged into the indigenous population and in the process, some of their own cultural traits became part of the culture of the Punjab. The present inhabitants of the Punjab are the descendants of the various racial stocks which entered into it during the different stages of its history.

Sikh Jats, who belong to the agriculturists class, form the bulk of population of the present Punjabis. They are sturdy, self-willed and industrious and are among the finest peasants of India. They are generally tall and muscular, with well-shaped limbs, an erect carriage and strongly marked and sharp handsome features.

The Khatris and Aroras are next in number. The Khatris, who are generally energetic and educated, are mostly fair-complexioned and have good features. Trade is their main occupation. They claim to be in the direct line of the Kshatriyas of the Aryan race. The Aroras also claim to be of Khatri origin. Next to them in number are the Brahmans and Vaishas, who are split up into several such-castes and are found almost all over Punjab.

Among the minor agricultural tribes, Sainis and Kambohs are the most prominent ones. They are admirable cultivators, skilful and industrious. The Sainis claim their origin from the Rajputs and some of the Kambohs from "Kamboj Desh" in

Afghanistan. The various vagrant tribes of the Punjab, like the Sainis, the Pakhi- Waras, the Bawris, the Bazigars etc. are aboriginal in their origin. They have retained their aboriginal customs and beliefs.

Tribal Settlement

The population of the Punjab being heterogeneous consists of various tribes and classes. Members of each village or patti claim descent from a common ancestor, and even today in every village one clan dominates.

There are various tribes and clans settled in the Punjab. Among them Jats, Khatris, Aroras, Brahmans, Vaishas, Sainis, Kambohs and Sansis are the most prominent. The Jats of the Punjab are further divided into various clans, each one of which is found concentrated in groups of villages. The most important clans of Jats in Malwa are Sindhus and Sindhu Brars.

From the Sindhu clan sprang up the great Phulkian families of Patiala, Nabha, and Jind, and from the Brars the ruling family of Faridkot, which ruled the native states later merged into Punjab.

The Bhullar, clans of Jats, who claim to have sprung from the 'jata' or matted hair of Mahadev, are also concentrated mostly in Malwa. The principal Jat clans of Majha are Dhillon, Randhawa, Chahil and Sindhu. The Sindhus and Gills, who claim descent from the Raghobasi branch of the Suryvanshi Rajputs, are mostly settled in the Amristar and Jullandur districts. In the Doab districts the main Jat clans are Randhawa, Bains, Sandhu and Gill.

Among the non-agriculturist tribes of the Punjab, the Khatris, the Aroras, and the Vaishas are the most significant ones. Most of them are engaged in trade and commerce. The Khatris are sub-divided into many groups, the most significant among them being the Dhaighares, the Charzatis, the Punjzatis, the Chhezatis, the Sarins, the Bahris and the Khakhrains. The Bedis and the Sodhis belong to the Bunjahi tribe. Bedis are mostly found around Dera Baba Nanak and Gurdaspur, while the Sodhis are settled mostly at Anandpur and Hoshiarpur.

In west Punjab, before the partition, the Khatris were mostly concentrated in the Jhelum and Rawalpindi districts and the Aroras in Multan and Derajat Division, but now both are spread almost all over the Punjab. Sainis and Kambohs are primarily cultivators.

The Sainis are mostly found in Jullundur, Hoshiarpur, Gurdaspur and Rupar and the Kambohs is Patiala, Jullundur, Kapurthala, Amristar and Ferozepur. The Kambohs of Doab claim their descent from Raja Karan.

The Sansis are vagrant tribes and seldom settle for long in one place. They are found in considerable numbers in Ludhiana, Amristar and Gurdaspur. The Nat-Bazigars also wander about with their families and never settle down at one place.

Cultural Complexity

Not a single village in the Punjab is homogeneous. Every community has its own social customs which are different to some extent from those of others. Religion further determines this cultural difference and mode of living.

Even when a Jat and a Khatri are next-door neighbours, some of their cultural traits remain different from each other. The practice of widow remarriage, for instance, is accepted by Jats but it is almost a taboo among the Khatris.

The Jats and the Khatris are further sub-divided into many clans which have their characteristic differences in customs pertaining to birth, death, marriage, etc.

Then there are the erstwhile low-castes who differ from all the other people in their habits and social customs. Besides, the three geographical strips, Majha, Malwa and Doaba have certain local cultural traits.

It is marvelous that under all these peculiarities a thread of homogeneity binds the Punjabis together as a whole. The Greeks, the Scythians, the Parthians, the Huns, the Pathans and the Mughals came here, settled down and got woven into its cultural fabric.

Socio-Economic Structure

As the majority of its population is rural, village is the unit that determines the social and economic set up of the Punjab. Every village is linked in one way of another with the adjoining villages. Agriculture being the main occupation of the people, their economic dependence upon each other mainly pertains to their agricultural activities. All of them carpenters, blacksmiths, oilmen, sweepers and others invest their interests in agriculture. Carpenters and blacksmiths make and repair agricultural implements for the farmers. Labourers lend a hand at harvesting and in return get wages. Similarly, barbers, water-carriers, cobblers, potters and all others earn their living by serving the farmer in one way or another.

Many villages have grown up in the middle of large fields. A village in the Punjab generally springs up on the land of an ancestor, his offspring forming the nucleus. Many villages of Majha are divided into pattis, and each member of a patti is said to have descended from a common ancestor. In some villages each patti has its separate Panchayat to sort out is quarrels and bring about reconciliation. But in case of interpatti disputes, the Panchayat of the main village decides the issues.

Working classes like Labourers and backward classes like sweepers live in mud houses on the out skirts of the village, or in some remote corners. The artisans and craftsmen like, carpenters, blacksmiths, cobblers etc. have their own separate locality.

Although the villages of Punjab are inhabited by different castes and creeds, the people of one village do not marry into the same and in this respect each village in an exogamous unit. matrimonial relations are transacted in nearly villages only. If a distant village has to be chosen, it must be of the same geographical strip. In the urban there is no such consideration.

CUSTOMS AND TRADITION

In the Customs and tradition of Punjab, kinship plays a significant role. The Punjabis have a very vast range of it. Its pattern varies considerably from groups to group but the general mode of behaviour and attitude is more or less the same. Each relation has certain duties and responsibilities towards others in his group, in the day-to-day life, birth and marriage ceremonies, funerals and other social occasions. Different sets of terms are used for addressing the patrilineal and matrilineal kinfolk. The father's brother, is addressed as chacha, while the mother's brother is mama. Even the terms used for addressing the elder or younger agnatic kin are different. The father's elder brother is addressed as taya and the younger one as chacha.

Generally most of the kinsmen of a person reside in the same village, or in the adjoining villages. Because of the joint family system, the real brothers, even married ones, often live in the same household. There are some other agnates who generally reside in the same locality, or patti, participate in all social functions and exchange gifts.

Some of the cognates reside in the adjoining villages and very often they participate in social or festive occasions, like the initiation and marriage ceremonies, as also other occasions like funerals etc.

Kinship plays a very vital role in the social and cultural life of the people because most of the kin have to perform certain specified and obligatory functions on social occasions. Thus, for instance, the choora (red ivory bangles) which bride wears at her wedding has necessarily to come as a gift from her maternal uncle. The maternal uncle has to put the bangles on her forearm while going through certain rituals. Similarly the maternal grandparents must send their khat (bridal gift) to the girl on the occasion of marriage. This gift generally comprises a set of clothes, some jewellery and other household objects for the bride. At an initiation ceremony, like the first haircutting or wedding, each relative gives something in cash or kind according to his social standing or nearness of relation. The exchange of gifts is a prominent custom and keeps the kin, in a way, well-knit in the social fabric. Presence of all relatives at social functions is considered very essential and special efforts are made to patch up differences with all those with whom relations have been strained for some reason or the other.

The joint family system having been in vogue for ages, the entire responsibility for the maintenance of the household and of social relations falls upon the father. No one in the family can question his authority. Even in such personal matters as contracting a marriage, the father as the head of the family, has the ultimate say. After his death the patriarchal powers pass on to the eldest son who becomes the head of the family and its chief representative on all social occasions.

At home the head of the family inspires awe among the members. Younger members of the family dare not talk flippantly or joke in his presence, nor is it considered befitting for them to smoke or drink when he around. All conversation in his presence is conducted in Subdued voices. Daughters-in-law observe purdah when the father-in-law is present and it is generally understood that when he comes into the house, he would either cough aloud, or indicate in some other way that he is around, so that they may cover their faces and tone down their voices.

As a general rule, there is no direct conversation between the father-in-law and the daughter-in-law, but if a situation and an occasion necessitate it, it is brief to the extent of being monosyllabic, and the daughter-in-law is barely audible.

Purdah is observed before the husband's elder brother also. The same customary respect as is shown to the father-in-law is also shown to him. But the younger brother of the husband, the devar, enjoys a privileged position. He is free to talk, laugh and joke with the bhabi (brother's wife). Among some clans, there is a custom that when the bride is brought home, the husband's younger brother is the first person who lifts here veil and peeps at her face. In certain clans the eldest bhabi is given a status equal to that of the mother and she is treated with great respect. In Malwa, where the devar generally marries the widow of the elder brother, the relationship is very free.

Generally speaking, relations between the mother-in-law and the daughter-in-law are not very cordial in many families. A lot of friction is caused over the domestic chores and sometimes even small mistakes on the part of the daughter-in-law are made much of by the mother-in-law. The offended mother-in-law in her outburst does not spare even the parental family of the daughter in-law. However, although the position of the wife varies in different societies, the mother occupies a very respectable position everywhere in Punjab.

Relations among brothers are often very friendly and cordial. They are always out to help one another. The elder brother generally commands the same respect as is given to the father. But a great change comes in this behaviour when the brothers get married and their wives start wrangling on petty matters. Over the distribution of ancestral property sometimes the filial love and respect change into life-long enmity.

The relationship between a brother and a sister is the warmest and cleanest of all relations. Right from her childhood a sister idealises her brother. When she plays the folk games kikli and thaal with her friends, she sings praises of her brother. After marriage when she is in her husband's home, she always looks forward to the arrival of her brother, because whenever she goes to her parents on a customary visit, it is the brother who fetches her. She looks up to him as her sole protected and expects help from him when she is in difficulties.

The agnates who live in a separate house though in the same village are generally the brothers or first cousins of the head of the family. Relations with them are generally kept pleasant and they in their turn join in all sorts of festive as well as sad occasions. Regular dealings of exchange of cash and gifts are maintained with them on all festive occasions.

Relatives from the maternal side generally reside in the adjacent villages. Children are, as a matter of course, more attached to their maternal relatives.

Among many clans, eating or even drinking water in the house, of married daughter is taboo. It is believed that one who eats in the house of one's married daughter goes to hell. Among some, even elder brothers are not supposed to accept the hospitality of their married sisters, nor accept any gifts from her. However, there is no restriction on children accepting such gifts or hospitality. But now with the change of times people's views have changed and the rule has been relaxed.

Sometimes close friends and associates enter into a ritualistic relationship. They often exchange their turbans, and are known as pag-wat brothers. They go to a temple or a gurudwara, exchange turbans and eat from the same plate. It is quite an occasion and many near relatives are invited. This sort of ritualistic relationship is frequent. Sometimes even a girl ties rakhi on the wrist of a boy outside her own kin and makes him her dharam bhra (brother in faith). The approach to these ritual relationships is very serious and all obligations are as earnestly observed as in the case of real kin ties.

Among the villagers of the Punjab, there is an unusual sense of kinships. So relative terms of address are used by fellow-villagers unrelated by either real or ritual ties. In all social communication, modes of address are very respectable.

In elderly woman is always addressed as chachi or masi (aunt) and as elderly man as chacha or mama (uncle). Similarly boys and girls of the same age-group generally address one another as brother or sister. A daughter is the most privileged person, as she is given a daughter's status in every household of the village.

3

Government and Politics

INTRODUCTION

Punjab is governed through a parliamentary system of representative democracy. Each of the states of India possesses a parliamentary system of government, with a ceremonial state Governor, appointed by the President of India on the advice of the central government. The head of government is an indirectly elected Chief Minister who is vested with most of the executive powers. The term length of the government is five years. The state legislature, the Vidhan Sabha, is the unicameral Punjab Legislative Assembly, with 117 members elected from single-seat constituencies. The current Government was elected in the 2017 Assembly elections as Congress won 77 out of 117 Assembly seats and Amarinder Singh is the current Chief Minister. The state of Punjab is divided into five administrative divisions and twenty-two districts.

The capital of Punjab is Chandigarh, which also serves as the capital of Haryana and is thus administered separately as a Union Territory of India. The judicial branch of the state government is provided by the Punjab and Haryana High Court in Chandigarh.

Punjab Legislative Assemblybuilding

The main players in the politics of the state are the Indian National Congress and the Shiromani Akali Dal (with alliance Bharatiya Janata Party). The present government is headed by Amarinder Singh. President's rule has been imposed in Punjab 8 times so far, since 1950, for different reasons. In terms of the absolute number of days, Punjab was under President's rule for 3510 days, which is about 10 years. Much of this was in the 80s during the height of militancy in Punjab. Punjab was under President's rule for 5 continuous years from 1987 to 1992.

GOVERNMENT OF PUNJAB

The Government of Punjab also known as the State Government of Punjab , or locally as State Government, is the supreme governing authority of the Indian state of Punjab and its 22 districts. It consists of an executive, led by the Governor of Punjab, a judiciary and a legislative branch.

Like other states in India, the head of state of Punjab is the Governor, appointed by the President of India on the advice of the Central government. His or her post is largely ceremonial.

The Chief Minister is the head of government and is vested with most of the executive powers. Chandigarh is the capital of Punjab, and houses the Vidhan Sabha (Legislative Assembly) and the secretariat. Chandigarh also serves as the capital of Haryana, and is a union territory of India. The Punjab & Haryana High Court, located in Chandigarh, has jurisdiction over the whole state.

The present Legislative Assembly of Punjab is unicameral, consisting of 117 Member of the Legislative Assembly (M.L.A). Its term is 5 years, unless sooner dissolved.

PUNJAB LEGISLATIVE ASSEMBLY

The Punjab Legislative Assembly or the Punjab Vidhan Sabha is the unicameral legislature of the state of Punjab in northern India. At present, it consists of 117 members, directly elected from 117 single-seat constituencies. The tenure of the Legislative Assembly is five years unless dissolved sooner. The current Speaker of the Assembly is Rana KP Singh. The meeting place of the Legislative Assembly since 6 March 1961 is the *Vidhan Bhavan* in Chandigarh. The current ruling party is the Indian National Congress with 2/3rd Majority .

History

British Raj

An Executive Council was formed under The Indian Councils Act, 1861. It was only under the Government of India Act 1919 that a Legislative Council was set up in Punjab. Later, under the Government of India Act 1935, the Punjab Legislative Assembly was constituted with a membership of 175. It was summoned for the first time on 1 April 1937. In 1947, Punjab Province was partitioned into West Punjab and East Punjab and the East Punjab Legislative Assembly was formed, the forerunner of the current assembly consisting of 72 members.

1947 – present

On 15 July 1948, eight princely states of East Punjab grouped together to form a single state, Patiala and East Punjab

States Union. The Punjab State Legislature was a bicameral house in April 1952, comprising the Vidhan Sabha (lower house) and Vidhan Parishad(upper house). In 1956 the state was reorganized and renamed Punjab, the strength of the Vidhan Parishad of the new State of Punjab was enhanced from 40 seats to 46 seats and in 1957, it was increased to 51. Punjab was trifurcated in 1966 to form Haryana, Himachal Pradesh, and Punjab. The Vidhan Parishad was reduced to 40 seats and the Vidhan Sabha was grown by 50 seats to 104 seats. On 1 January 1970, the Vidhan Parishad was abolished leaving the state with a unicameral legislature.

Current Speaker of the Vidhan Sabha (Legislative Assembly)

Rana KP Singh (Rana Kanwar Pal Singh) is the current Speaker of the Punjab Legislative Assembly. He was born in Jhandian village in Rupnagar in 1957. Rana K P Singh completed his schooling in neighboring Bharatgarh before moving to Dehradun to study law. He practiced law in Rupnagar courts for 21 years. After becoming sarpanch of his village, he was elevated to the position of the Youth Congress district president. Later, he became the general secretary of the Indian National Congress, Punjab unit before becoming a member of the All India Congress Committee. Key Positions Held:

- Chairman, Sri Anandpur Sahib Land Development Bank
- President, District Bar Association, Rupnagar
- Chairman, Punjab Pollution Control Board, Punjab Govt.
- Parliamentary Secretary, Punjab Govt.
- Senator, Panjab University
- Member of Public Accounts Committee of 12th Punjab Legislative Assembly during the years 2002-03 and 2004-05.
- Chairman, Committee on Questions and References and Member of Committee on Estimates of 12th Punjab Legislative Assembly during the year 2003-04.
- Member of Committee on Subordinate Legislation and

Committee on Petitions of Punjab Legislative Assembly during the year 2004-05.

- Member of Committee on Public Undertakings, Public Accounts Committee, Committee on Government Assurances, Committee on Papers laid/to be laid on the Table of the House, Committee on Estimates and House Committee during the years 2007-2012.

He was re-elected to the state assembly from Anandpur Sahib in 2017. Presently, he is serving as Speaker of Punjab Legislative Assembly elected by the members of the house unanimously on 27.03.2017

POLITICS OF PUNJAB

Politics in reorganised present-day Punjab is dominated by mainly two parties. One is Shiromani Akali Dal(Badal) and the other is Indian National Congress. Since 1967, Chief Minister of Punjab has been predominantly from Jat Sikh community despite its 21 percent state population. Only exception was Giani Zail Singh, the Chief Minister of Punjab from 17 March 1972 to 30 April 1977 belonging to Other Backward Class (Ramgarhia OBC) community that has population of 31.3 percent. However Scheduled Castes (Dalit) community never had Chief Minister from community or proper representation in Government, despite having 32 percent population in the state.

Other prominent party is Bahujan Samaj Party especially in Doaba region. In 1992 BSP won 9 seats Vidhan Sabha elections. Also BSP won 3 lok sabha seats from Punjab in 1996 general elections and only Garhshanker seat in 1997 Vidhan Sabha elections. Communist parties too have some influence in the Malwa area. In the 2014 general elections, the first-time contesting Aam Aadmi Party got 4 out of 13 seats in Punjab by winning 34 of the total 117 assembly segments, coming second in 7, third in 73 and fourth in the rest 3 segments.The support for the Aam Aadmi Party increased later in Punjab. The current Government was elected in the 2017 Punjab Assembly elections and the Congress won 77 out of 117 Assembly seats with Captain Amarinder Singh as the current Chief Minister. The AAP, fighting its first assembly election in the state, won 20 seats. The incumbent BJP-SAD alliance came third with 18 seats.

History

Pre-1947 period

Before 1947 partition of Punjab, politics were dominated by Unionist Party as it was main party in united Punjab especially seen in 1937 elections.

1947–1966

During 1947-1966 Punjab was undivided and consisted of present-day Punjab, Haryana, Himachal Pradesh, and Chandigarh. This meant that both population and religion factor of whole state was mixed and politics were dominated by Indian National Congress.

Political parties

Punjab has many political parties but only five parties recognized by Election Commission of India and having presence in the state:

- Three National parties in Punjab are Indian National Congress, Bhartiya Janta Party and Bahujan Samaj Party.
- Two recognized state parties in Punjab are Aam Aadmi Party and Shiromani Akali Dal.

POLITICAL PARTIES

Traditonally the Akali Dal and the Congress have been the two parties that have been in power in the Punjab state of India. In the early years after independence Congress's Pratap Singh Kairon dominated Punjab as a C. M. He also did most of the infrastructure building that brought Punjab it's prosperity as all the fabled irrigation system was in Pakistani Punjab. Early on the Akali's were not a force but with time they too became politically active.

This brought religion into Punjab politics and the Central Congress party's attmepts to counter this through Bhinderanwala caused the state to have religious militancy, caused by small section of Sikh separatists, through most of the decade of the 1980's.

The Akalis had leaders who were ambivalent on the Khalistan issue but as a party recovered from the prolonged President's rule in Punjab in the 1980's by allying with the BJP.

All India Netaji Revolutionary Party

All India Netaji Revolutionary Party, was a political party in India. AINRP was led by V.P. Saini, who is also the president of the Netaji Research Foundation.

The party was founded in connection with the 5th All India Netaji Convention 1999. The party was formed in order to work the ideology of Netaji Subhash Chandra Bose. The party demanded a through investigastion into what happened to Netaji Subhas Chandra Bose, about whom the circumstances of his death are still unclear.

AINRP was critical of the collaboration of the left (CPI(M) and All India Forward Bloc) with the Indian National Congress. In the Lok Sabha elections of 1999 V.P. Saini was launched as a candidate in the constituency of Hoshiarpur in Punjab. Saini only got 942 votes (0,16%).

Later Saini joined All India Forward Bloc, and became the secretary of the central committee. In 2003, Saini visited North Korea as part of an AIFB-delegation from Punjab.

Bahujan Samaj Party (Kainth)

Bahujan Samaj Party (Kainth), a splinter group of Bahujan Samaj Party in Punjab. BSP(K) was founded on October 30, 2004. BSP(K) is led by Satnam Singh Kainth (ex MP and ex-president of Democratic Bahujan Samaj Morcha). Kainth had re-joined BSP ahead of the 2004 Lok Sabha elections, but was later expelled.

Bharti Lok Lehar Party

Bharati Lok Lehar Party, political party in the Indian state of Punjab. The party was founded in February 2004, as a break-away from the Bahujan Samaj Party. The founders of BLLP had been leaders of the Democratic Bahujan Samaj Morcha, which had merged with BSP. The party works for the interests of dalits. The party leader is Manohar Lal Mahey.

Dalit Kisan Dal

Dalit Kisan Dal (Dalit Peasants Party), is a political party in Punjab, India.

The party was formed as a splinter-group from Lok Bhalai Party 2001, when activists from LBP in Khamano, Machhiwara, Ropar and Samrala broke away. The general secretary of DKD is Bhinder Singh Ranwan, and the party president is Iqbal Singh Kapurthala. The party claims to fight for better conditions for peasants and dalits.

Democratic Bahujan Samaj Morcha

Democratic Bahujan Samaj Morcha (Democratic Majority Society Front) was a political party in India, based in the state of Punjab. DBSM was formed on 20 December 1997 as a break-away from Bahujan Samaj Party, in protest to the alliance of BSP with the Indian National Congress in the state. DBSM was led by Satnam Singh Kainth. DBSM allied themselves with Shiromani Akali Dal and BJP.

In the Lok Sabha elections 1999, DBSM put up Satnam Singh Kainth as a candidate in Phillaur in Punjab, backed by SAD-BJP. Kainth came second with 236 962 votes (38,61%).

In the state elections in Punjab 2002 DBSM launched two candidates, backed by SAD-BJP, who got 23 664 (29,86%) and 10 372 votes (13,25%).

DBSM was reunified with BSP in 2004, but important sectors opposed the merger. Those broke away and formed Bharti Lok Lehar Party.

General Samaj Party

General Samaj Party is a political party in the Indian state of Punjab. GSP was founded in 2002. GSP opposes affirmative action quotas.

The general secretary of the party is T. N. Sharma. The Punjab state general secretary is Rajbir Singh Sidhu. The president of the party is Suresh Kumar Goyal. The convenor of the Yuva Morcha (Youth Front) of the party is Bhupinder Bansal.

In March 2003 GSP won one of 21 seats in the Gurdaspur Municipal Corporation.

Lok Sangharsh Morcha

Lok Sangharsh Morcha (People's Struggle Front), a front organization of the Ram Pasla-led fraction of Communist Party of India (Marxist) in Punjab. The front existed in 2000. Pasla's fraction later broke away from CPI(M) after Pasla's expulsion in 2001. The convenor of the front is Tarsem Jodha, a former CPI(M) Punjab legislator and leading member of Pasla's party

Punjab Communist Revolutionary Committee

Punjab Communist Revolutionary Committee, originally the Bhatinda District Committee of AICCCR. The committee was one of the sections that broke away when AICCCR founded CPI(M-L). In June 1976 PCRC merged with UCCRI(ML).

Punjab Janata Morcha

Punjab Janata Morcha (Punjab Popular Front), a Sikh political party in the Indian state of Punjab. The general secretary of PJM is Gian Chand.

In November 1997 PJM took part in the foundation of Committee for Coordination on Disappearances in Punjab.

In December 2001 PJM joined the Panthic Morcha, a front of anti-Badal groups.

PJM was opposed to the government of BJP.

Punjab Lok Congress Party

Punjab Lok Congress Party, a political party in Punjab, India. PLC was formed by Nationalist Congress Party Ludhiana Rural District chief Rashpal Singh Gill. PLC was founded on March 12, 2002, following the poor performance of NCP in the 2002 Punjab state assembly elections.

Purvanchal Vikas Party

Purvanchal Vikas Party, a political party in the Indian state of Punjab founded in 2004. PVP is active amongst the migrant labourers in and around the city of Ludhiana. Amongst other issues, PVP demands the construction of a Purvanchal Bhavan for migrant labourers.

The convenor of the party (until a regular conference is held) is T. R. Misra.

Rashtriya Raksha Dal

Rashtriya Raksha Dal (National Defence Party), a political party in India, mainly based in Punjab. The party was founded on August 7, 1999, and works for the conditions of army veterans. The All India General Secretary of the party is Lt. Col. Adish Pal Singh Jhabal.

Reservation Virodhi Dal

Reservation Virodhi Dal (Antireservation Party) a political party in the Indian state of Punjab. The party was floated in October 1999 by the General Category Welfare Federation of Punjab. The party is opposed to affirmative action quotas and reservations. The convenor of the party is Raghunandan Singh.

Revolutionary Communist Centre of India (Maoist)

Revolutionary Communist Centre of India (Maoist), was a communist group based in Punjab. RCCI(M) was formed in 1995, as the Revolutionary Communist Centre of India (Marxist-Leninist) was divided into two (the other faction was the

Revolutionary Communist Centre of India (Marxist-Leninist-Maoist)). The secretary of RCCI(M) was Shamsher Singh Sheri.

RCCI(M) held conferences in 1996 and 2002.

RCCI(M) was a candidate member of Revolutionary Internationalist Movement (RIM). It was also one of the founding organisations of the Coordination Committee of Maoist Parties and Organisations of South Asia. In January 2003, RCCI(M) merged with Maoist Communist Centre, which then took the name Maoist Communist Centre of India.

Shiromani Akali Dal

Akali Dal, also termed as Shiromani Akali Dal (*Akali Religious Party*), is a Sikh political party mainly based in Punjab, India.

It was formed on 13 December 1920 after the formation of SGPC (Shiromani Gurudwara Prabandhak Committee), a religious body formed as a result of movement to secure Sikh Gurdwaras from corrupt priests. So in a sense Akali Dal considers itself as a religio-political party and principal representative of Sikhs. Sardar Gurmukh Singh Chubbal was the first president of the Akali Dal but it was under Master Tara Singh that Akali Dal became a force to reckon with.

They launched Punjabi Suba agitation to get a Sikh majority state made from undivided Punjab based on language under the leadership of Sant Fateh Singh. In 1966, Punjab was formed but its division led to bitter conflict as neither parties were satisfied. Akali Dal came to power in Punjab but many a times their governments were dismissed by the Congress Party ruling at the federal level.

The Dal's chief opponent in the state is the Indian National Congress. Its political ally in the state and at the Centre is the Hindutva Bharatiya Janata Party. Since Punjab is about 65% Sikh, the SAD needs the support of as many Hindus as the BJP can get to form lasting administrations, and the BJP needs the SAD to bring as many parliamentary seats from Punjab as it can to form a Union government.

Akali Dal's history is also full of divisions and factionalism. Each faction claims to be the real Akali Dal. As of 2003, the SAD headed by Parkash Singh Badal was the largest faction and the one recognized as having the name SAD by the Election Commission of India. Other factions have included Sarb Hind Shiromani Akali Dal led by Gurcharan Singh Tohra, Shiromani Akali Dal (Simranjit Singh Mann) (also called SAD (Amritsar)), and Shiromani Akali Dal (Panthik) led by Amarinder Singh (which later merged with Congress), Shiromani Akali Dal Delhi, Shiromani Akali Dal (Democratic), Haryana State Akali Dal and the Shiromani Akali Dal (Longowal).

In the fall of 2003 the Badal and Tohra factions reunified.

The basic philosophy of Akali Dal is to give political voice to Sikh issues (Panthic cause) and it believes that religion and politics go hand in hand.

At the February 2007 Punjab state elections, the Shiromani Akali Dal won 48 of the 117 seats, becoming the largest party in the Assembly. The alliance of the SAD and BJP took over the state government from the Congress Party, with Baidal as chief minister.

Shiromani Akali Dal (Amritsar)

Shiromani Akali Dal (Amritsar), registered with the Election Commission of India as Shiromani Akali Dal (Simranjit Singh Mann), a splinter group of the Shiromani Akali Dal led by Simranjit Singh Mann.

The Shiromani Akali Dal (Amritsar) advocates the independence of Punjab via recognition of the Punjabi peoples' right to self-determination.

Shiromani Akali Dal (Democratic)

Shiromani Akali Dal (Democratic), a splinter group of the Badal-led Shiromani Akali Dal. SAD(D) was formed in 1996. Party president was Kuldip Singh Wadala.

SAD(D) joined the Punjab Loktantrik Morcha together with Marxist Communist Party of India, Samajwadi Party,

Samajwadi Janata Party (Rashtriya), Janata Dal (Secular), Republican Party of India and Punjab Milkman Union.

Ahead of the 2004 Lok Sabha elections SAD(D) merged with the Badal-led Shiromani Akali Dal.

Shiromani Akali Dal (Longowal)

Shiromani Akali Dal (Longowal) is a splinter group of the Badal-led Shiromani Akali Dal. The party was launched on June 7, 2004. Its president is Prem Singh Chandumajra (formerly general secretary of Sarb Hind Shiromani Akali Dal) from Patiala. In the 2004 Lok Sabha elections the party contested the Patiala seat, but failed.

Shiromani Akali Dal (Panthic)

Shiromani Akali Dal (Panthic), a hard-line splinter group of Shiromani Akali Dal (Simranjit Singh Mann)). SAD(P) was formed in 1990. It is led by Jasbir Singh Rode.

Shiromani Akali Dal (Panthik)

Shiromani Akali Dal (Panthik), a Sikh political party in the Indian state of Punjab. One of several splinter groups of Shiromani Akali Dal.

SAD (Panthik) was launched by Amarinder Singh in 1991. Singh was an Akali moderate, who opposed the Khalistani militancy.

In January 1992 SAD (Panthik) merged with the Shiromani Akali Dal (Longowal). Amarinder however felt marginalized, and in February 1997 the SAD (Panthik) was re-launched.

On September 12 1997 SAD (Panthik) merged with the Indian National Congress.

Unionist Muslim League

The Unionist Muslim League, also known simply as the Unionist party was a political party based in the province of Punjab during British Raj in India. The Unionist party mainly represented the interests of the landed gentry and landlords of Punjab, which included Muslims, Hindus and Sikhs. However, the party was an umbrella organisation of the All India Muslim League. The Unionists dominated the political scene in Punjab from World War I to the independence of India and Pakistan in 1947.

Organisation

The Unionist party, like Congress a secular Party, was formed as a political party representing the interests of Punjab's large feudal classes and gentry.Although a majority of Unionists were Muslims, a large number of Hindus and Sikhs also supported and participated in the Unionist party.

This was in contrast to the Indian National Congress and other socialist political parties that adopted a mass-based approach.

In contrast to the Congress, in its early years of establishment, the Unionists supported the British Raj.

The Unionists contested elections for the Punjab Legislative Council and the Imperial Legislative Council, which were boycotted by the Congress and the Muslim League.

Thus Unionist members composed a majority of Punjab's legislators and council members for several decades.

Link with the Muslim League

The Unionists shared a common constitution with the Muslim League and followed a common policy and agenda for national issues.

But the Unionist organisation and activities in Punjab were virtually independent of the League. The Unionists were virtually an independent political party in the 1920s and 1930s, when the Muslim League was unpopular and divided into feuding factions.

The links improved after Muhammad Ali Jinnah became the League's president in the mid-1930s. However, the rule of Unionist leader Sir Sikander Hyat Khan was undisputed in the Punjab. Sir Sikander served numerous terms as Punjab's chief minister, often forming alliances with the Congress and the Shiromani Akali Dal despite Jinnah's opposition to both parties.

Sir Sikander remained the most popular and influential politician in Punjab during his lifetime, preventing both Jinnah and Sir Muhammad Iqbal from gaining the support of a majority of Punjabi Muslims.

PUNJAB LEGISLATIVE ASSEMBLY ELECTION, 2017

A Legislative Assembly election was held in the Indian state of Punjab on 4 February 2017 to elect the 117 members of the Punjab Legislative Assembly.

The counting of votes was done on 11 March 2017. The ruling pre-election coalition was the alliance comprising the political parties Shiromani Akali Dal and Bharatiya Janata Party and led by Chief Minister Parkash Singh Badal.

The voter turnout for the Punjab Assembly election was 76.83%. The Indian National Congress led by former Chief Minister Captain Amarinder Singh defeated the rulling alliance and the new comer Aam Aadmi Party.

Background

Electoral process changes

In April 2016, the Election Commission of India revealed about 8 lakh bogus votes of state being cancelled in the past one year and over 7 lakh youngsters who have attained the age of 18 this year were yet to get registered.

One constituency in every district will be chosen for trial run of Voter-verified paper audit trail (VVPAT) machines used along with EVMs.

Election Commission also decided to set up new polling stations if the number of voters was more than 1200 in rural areas and 1400 in urban areas.

33 constituencies of all district headquarters in Punjab had VVPAT machines installed with EVMs, including 22 district headquarters besides 11 high-profile constituencies.

Assembly constituencies of Punjab having VVPAT facility with EVMs

Lambi	Jalalabad	Majitha	Patiala
Atam Nagar	Chabbewal	Guruharsahai	Ferozpur
Barnala	Sanour	Lehragaga	Jalandhar (central)
Bathinda (urban)	Raikot	Moga	Anandpur Sahib
Bholath	Qadian	Chabbewal	Rampura Phul

As per the special summary revision of electoral rolls, there are a total of 1.9 crore voters in Punjab as of August 2016.

Final voters list for Punjab Legislative Assembly election 2017

S.No	Group of voters	Voters population
1	Male	1.05 crore
2	Female	94 lakhs

Total Voters 1.9 crore

Political developments

The 2014 general election was held in Punjab for 13 parliamentary constituencies. Shiromani Akali Dal and Aam Aadmi Party won 4 seats each, Congress won 3, and 2 constituencies elected Bharatiya Janata Party candidates. The first-time contesting Aam Aadmi Party won from 34 of the total 117 assembly segments, coming second in 7, third in 73 and fourth in the rest 3 segments. Wherever it trailed the major parties its vote share was mostly bigger than the margin of victory of the winning candidate, turning forthcoming elections into three-cornered contests.

Shiromani Akali Dal-Bharatiya Janata Party

The previous election, held in 2012, resulted in a majority of seats being won by ruling Shiromani Akali Dal-Bharatiya Janata Party and Parkash Singh Badal became Chief Minister of Punjab.

Aam Aadmi Party

In December 2015, Aam Aadmi Party declared that it would contest the Legislative Assembly elections in 2017. AAP which did not participate in the previous assembly election, had fought 2014 lok sabha elections. Their 2014 performance translates to 33 assembly seats out of 117. The performance of AAP was below expectations and 25 candidates of the party lost their deposit amounts.

Indian National Congress

The Congress will take part in the elections under the leadership of Amarinder Singh, and the party has hired poll strategist Prashant Kishor for campaigning.

Bahujan Samaj Party

The BSP is the fourth largest party in Punjab after improving its vote share in 2012 elections started preparations for 2017 early by launching *Punjab Bachao Abhiyaan* from 1 November 2014. In 2012, the BSP came second from Balachaur Vidhan sabha seat with 21943 votes. On 15 March 2016, Mayawati during a mega-rally in Nawanshahr on the birth anniversary of BSP founder Kanshi Ram in Punjab attacked SAD-BJP government as 'anti-Dalit' and Arvind Kejriwal as a "baniya" who had "always worked against Dalit and Scheduled Caste people" before he became Delhi CM.

Mayawati also declared that the BSP will contest Punjab 2017 elections on its own in all 117 seats. The BSP declared that it will root out the drug menace from the state within a month of coming to power in Punjab. In 9 June 2016, BSP national president Mayawati supported the film on Punjab drug abuse *Udta Punjab*, saying there is 'nothing wrong' in it. In May 2016, the BSP launched the *Pind Pind Chalo, Ghar Ghar Chalo* campaign, a door-to-door driveto to cover 29 million people across 550,000 households with *Punjab Bachao, BSP laao* (Save Punjab, elect BSP) as its main slogan as well as the overall theme of the campaign. The BSP formed 65 teams for around 15,000 big and small rallies as well as seminars to be conducted in the state. The party also announced a 10 percent reservation for the poor *upper castes* if the BSP government comes to power in Punjab. BSP Punjab unit started social media campaigning and also visited NRIs for support in Vienna, Europe and North America. On 16 May 2016, the Ambedkar Sena Punjab merged with BSP. Gurmel Chander, former president of The SC & BC teachers employees Union, joined the BSP on 25 August. On 25 September 2016, the BSP announced a list of nine candidates for 2017 Punjab assembly elections. On 25 September 2016, Avtar Singh Karimpuri was replaced with Rashpal Singh Raju as BSP Punjab state president as the former was declared a Vidhan Sabha candidate from Phillaur. Karimpuri's entry in Phillaur constituency has spiced up the political battle in the seat. Karimpuri said that the Punjab Congress does not want an alliance with the BSP, rather its agenda was to wipe out BSP from Punjab in the 2017 assembly elections. New BSP president Rashpal Raju announced a mega-rally in Phagwara on 9 October Parinirvana divas of BSP founder Kanshi Ram. At this rally Avtar Singh Karimpuri and Dr Megh Raj attacked Shiromani Akali Dal and Congress as anti-Sikh parties.

Election issues

First and foremost issue is Drug peddling, There are several election issues like unemployment & lack of skills, farmers' crises, continually failing economy, *sifarish* (patronage & influence peddling & nepotism), unbridled crime and the role of goons in day-to-day matters of the citizen, road rage & accidents, Atrocities against Dalits and dalit land issues in Sangrur area, the 1984 anti-Sikh riots and the supply of drugs & addiction to them. Punjabi Non-resident Indians (NRIs) play a major role in elections.

Caste and religion data

As per the 2011 census, 57.69% of the state's population follows Sikhism, making Punjab the only Sikh majority state in India. Hindus form 38.5% of the population, while Muslims,

1.93%; Christians, 1.3%; Buddhists, 0.12%; and Jains, 0.16%. Dalits (Scheduled Castes) constitute 31.94% of the population, the highest percentage amongst all the states. Other Backward Classes (OBCs) like -Sainis, Sunar, Kambojs, Tarkhans/ Ramgarhias, Gurjars, Kumhars/Prajapatis, Telis, Banjaras, Lohars constitute 20%- 25% of the population. Jat-Sikhs comprise 21% of the population while other forward castes (general category) - Brahmins, Khatris/Bhapas, Bania, Thakurs/ Rajputs constitute around 20%. As of 2016, Government of India has not publicly released Socio Economic and Caste Census 2011 *caste population data* for every single non-SC/ST castes (General castes, OBC/EBCs) in India.

LAW AND ORDER SET-UP

Punjab state law and order is maintained by Punjab Police. Punjab police is headed by its DGP, Suresh Arora, and has 70,000 employees. It manages state affairs through 22 district heads known as SSP.

Administrative set-up

Punjab has 22 districts which are geographically classified into Majha, Malwa, Doaba and Poadh regions. They are officially divided among 5 divisions: Patiala, Rupnagar, Jalandhar, Faridkot and Firozepur.

Majha

- Amritsar
- Tarn Taran
- Gurdaspur
- Pathankot

Doaba

- Hoshiarpur
- Kapurthala
- Jalandhar
- Shaheed Bhagat Singh Nagar(Nawanshahr)

Malwa

- Barnala
- Bathinda
- Ferozepur
- Fazilka
- Faridkot
- Ludhiana
- Moga
- Mansa
- Muktsar
- Patiala
- Sangrur

Each district under the administrative control of a District Collector. The districts are subdivided into 79 tehsils, which have fiscal and administrative powers over settlements within their borders, including maintenance of local land records comes under the administrative control of a Tehsildar. Each Tehsil consists of blocks which are total 143 in number. The blocks consist of revenue villages. There are total number of revenue villages in the state is 12,278. There are 22 Zila Parishads, 136 Municipal Committees and 22 Improvement Trusts looking after 143 towns and 14 cities of Punjab. Majitha is newly created tehsil, which was formed in September 2016. Zirakpur is the latest sub-tehsil, in the district of Mohali.

The capital and largest city of the state is Chandigarh. Out of total population of Punjab, 37.48% people live in urban regions. The absolute urban population living in urban areas is 10,399,146 of which 5,545,989 are males and while remaining 4,853,157 are females. The urban population in the last 10 years has increased by 37.48 percent. The major cities are Ludhiana, Amritsar, Jalandhar, Patiala, Bathinda, Sangrur, and SAS Nagar (Mohali).

4

Language and Literature

LANGUAGE

It is an Indo-European language within the Indic branch of the Indo-Iranian subfamily. Unusually for an Indo-European language, Punjabi is tonal; the tones arose as a reinterpretation of different consonant series in terms of pitch. In terms of morphological complexity, it is an agglutinative language (also very unusual for an Indo-European language, most of which are inflecting) and words are usually ordered 'Subject Object Verb'.

The Punjabi people suffered a split between India and Pakistan during the Partition of 1947. Punjabi is also one of the several languages spoken in the Indian subcontinent.

Dialects and Geographic Distribution

Punjabi is the official language of the Indian state of Punjab and the shared state capital Chandigarh. It is one of the second official languages of Delhi and Haryana. It is also spoken in neighbouring areas such as Kashmir and Himachal Pradesh. Punjabi is the predominantly spoken language in the Punjab province of Pakistan (and the most widely spoken language in Pakistan according to the CIA factbook), although it has no official status there, and both Urdu and English are preferred languages of the elite.

Punjabi is also spoken as a minority language in several other countries where Punjabis have emigrated in large numbers such as the United States, Australia, the United Kingdom (where it is the second most commonly used language) and Canada (where it is the fifth most commonly used language). Punjabi is the preferred language of the Sikhs because much of their religious literature is written in a similar language. It is the usual language of Bhangra music, which has recently gained wide popularity both in South Asia and abroad.

There are many dialects of Punjabi and they all form part of a dialect continuum, merging with Sindhi and related languages in Pakistan, and Hindustani in India. The main dialects of Punjabi are Majhi, Doabi, Malwai and Powadhi in India, and Pothohari, Lahndi and Multani in Pakistan. Majhi is the standard written form of Punjabi and is the dialect used in both Amritsar and Lahore.

The Punjabi University, Patiala, lists the following as dialects of Punjabi:

Some of these dialects, such as Dogri, Siraiki and Hindko are sometimes considered separate languages, and are classified in different zones or divisions of Indo-Aryan:

- Eastern (Central Zone): Bhattiani (a mixture of Panjabi and Rajasthani), Powadhi, Doabi, Malwai, Majhi, Bathi
- Western (Northwestern Zone, Lahndi): Multani, Hindko, Pahari, Pothohari
- Northern Zone: Dogri

As classified in SIL Ethnologue:

Western Literature

Many sources subdivide the Punjabi language into Western Punjabi or Lahndi, and Eastern Punjabi. They tend to do so based on GA Grierson's Linguistic Survey of India. The decision to divide the language has been controversial. The exact division of the language and even the legitimacy of such a division is disputed.

The dialect spoken in central Punjab—on both the Indian and Pakistani side—is Majhi. Grierson defined Western Punjabi as being west of a line running north-south from Montgomery and Gujranwala districts. This is well within present day Pakistan. Contrary to this, Ethnologue has come to classify Lahndi as the dialect of Punjabi spoken in all of Pakistan.

Vocabulary

Modern Punjabi vocabulary has been influenced by other languages, including Urdu, Hindi, Persian, Arabic, Sanskrit and English.

Much like English, Punjabi has moved around the world and developed local forms by integrating local vocabulary. While most loanwords come from Urdu, Hindi, Persian and English, Punjabi emigrants around the world have integrated terms from such languages as Spanish and Dutch. A distinctive "Diaspora Punjabi" is thus emerging. As there is no formal consensus over vocabulary and spelling in Punjabi, it is likely that Diaspora Punjabi will increasingly deviate from the forms found on the Indian Subcontinent in the future.

Writing System

There are several different scripts used for writing the Punjabi language, depending on the region and the dialect spoken, as well as the religion of the speaker. The script used for writing Punjabi in the Punjab province of Pakistan is known as Shahmukhi (*from the mouth of the Kings*) which is a modified version of Persian-Nasta'liq script. Sikhs and others in the Indian state of Punjab tend to use the Gurmukhi (*from the mouth of the Gurus*) script. Hindus, and those living in neighbouring states such as Haryana and Himachal Pradesh sometimes use the Devanagari script. Gurmukhi and Shahmukhi scripts are the most commonly used for writing Punjabi and are considered the official scripts of the language.

Gurmukhi Script

The Gurmukhi script is derived from the Later Sharada script and was standardized by the second Sikh *guru*, Guru Angad Dev, in the 16th century for writing the Punjabi language. The whole of the Guru Granth Sahib's 1430 pages are written in this script. The name *Gurmukhi* is derived from the Old Punjabi term "Guramukhi", meaning "from the mouth of the Guru".

Gurmukhi is a system of writing called an abugida, where each consonant has an inherent vowel (a) that can be changed using vowel signs.

Modern Gurmukhi has forty-one consonants (*vianjan*), nine vowel symbols (*laga matra*), two symbols for nasal sounds (*bindi* and *mippi*), and one symbol which duplicates the sound of any consonant (*addak*). In addition, four conjuncts are used: three subjoined forms of the consonants Rara, Haha and Vava, and one half-form of Yayya. Use of the conjunct forms of Vava and Yayya is increasingly scarce in modern contexts.

Gurmukhi has been adapted to write other languages, such as Braj Bhasha, Khariboli (and other Hindustani dialects), Sanskrit and Sindhi.

Origins

Like most of the North Indian writing systems, the Gurmukhi script is a descendant of the Brahmi script. The *Proto-Gurmukhi letters* evolved through the Gupta script, from 4th to 8th century, followed by the Sharada script, from 8th century onwards, and finally adapted their archaic form in the *Devasesha* stage of the Later Sharada script, dated between the 10th and 14th centuries.

The traditional accounts, such as the references found in the *Janamsakhi* literature, say that the Gurmukhi script was invented by the second Sikh Guru, Guru Angad Dev. However, it would be correct to say that the script was standardised, rather than invented, by the Sikh Gurus. E. P. Newton (*Panjabi Grammar*, 1898) writes that at least 21 Gurmukhi characters are found in ancient manuscripts: 6 from 10th century, 12 from 3rd century BC and 3 from 5th century BC. Apparently, the first Sikh Guru, Guru Nanak Dev also used the Gurmukhi script for his writings.

There are two major theories on how the *Proto-Gurmukhi script* emerged in the 15th century. G. B. Singh (1950), while quoting Abu Raihan Al-Biruni's *Ta'rikh al-Hind* (1030 AD), says that the script evolved from Ardhanagari. Al-Biruni writes that the Ardhanagari script was used in Bathinda, including Sindh and western parts of the Punjab in the 10th century.

For some time, Bhatinda remained the capital of the kingdom of Bhatti Rajputs of the Pal clan, who ruled North India before the Muslims occupied the country. Because of its connection with the Bhattis, the Ardhanagari script was also called Bhatachhari. According to Al-Biruni, Ardhanagari was a mixture of Nagari, used in Ujjain and Malwa, and *Siddha Matrika* or the Siddham script, a variant of the Sharada script used in Kashmir.

Pritam Singh (1992) has also traced the origins of Gurmukhi to the *Siddha Matrika.*

Tarlochan Singh Bedi (1999) writes that the Gurmukhi script developed in the 10-14th centuries from the *Devasesha* stage of the Sharada script. His argument is that from the 10th century, regional differences started to appear between the Sharada script used in Punjab, the Hill States (partly Himachal Pradesh) and Kashmir. The regional Sharada script evolves from this stage till the 14th century, when it starts to appear in the form of Gurmukhi. Indian epigraphists call this stage Devasesha, while Bedi prefers the name *Pritham Gurmukhi* or Proto-Gurmukhi.

Gurus adopted the *Proto-Gurmukhi script* to write the Guru Granth Sahib, the religious scriptures of the Sikhs. Other contemporary scripts used in the Punjab were Takri and the LaG

- Alphabets also *Takri* was a script that developed through the *Devasesha* stage of the Sharada script, and is found mainly in the Hill States, such as Chamba, where it is called *Chambyali* and in Jammu, where it is known as *Dogri*. The local *Takri* variants got the status of official scripts in some of the Punjab Hill States, and were used for both administrative and literary purposes until the 19th century. After 1948, when Himachal Pradesh was established as an administrative unit, the local *Takri* variants were replaced by Devanagari.

- Meanwhile, the mercantile scripts of Punjab known as the LaG were normally not used for literary purposes. *Landa* means alphabet "without tail", applying that the script did not have vowel symbols. In Punjab, there were at least ten different scripts classified as LaG
- Mahajani being the most popular. The LaG
- Alphabets were used for household and trade purposes. Compared to the LaG
- Sikh Gurus favoured the use of *Proto-Gurmukhi*, because of the difficulties involved in pronouncing words without vowel signs.

The usage of Gurmukhi letters in Guru Granth Sahib meant that the script developed its own orthographical rules. In the following epochs, Gurmukhi became the prime script applied for literary writings of the Sikhs. Later in the 20th century, the script was given the authority as the official script of the Eastern Punjabi language. Meanwhile, in Western Punjab a form of the *Urdu script*, known as Shahmukhi is still in use.

Gurmukhi Etymology

The word *Gurmukhi* is commonly translated as "from the Mouth of the Guru". However, the term used for the *Punjabi script* has somewhat different connotations. The opinion given by traditional scholars is that as the Sikh holy writings, before they were scribed, were uttered by the Gurus, they came to be known as Gurmukhi or the "*Utterance* of the Guru".

And consequently, the script that was used for scribing the *utterance* was also given the same name. However, the prevalent view among Punjabi linguists is that as in the early stages the Gurmukhi letters were primarily used by *Gurmukhs*, or the Sikhs devoted to the Guru, the script came to be associated with them.

Vowels

Gurmukhi follows similar concepts to other Brahmi scripts and as such, all consonants are followed by an inherent 'a' sound (unless at the end of a word when the 'a' is usually dropped).

This inherent vowel sound can be changed by using dependent vowel signs which attach to a bearing consonant. In some cases, dependent vowel signs cannot be used – at the beginning of a word or syllable for instance– and so an independent vowel character is used instead.

Halant

The Halant character is not used when writing Punjabi in Gurmukhi. However, it may occasionally be used in Sanskritised text or in dictionaries for extra phonetic information. When it is used, it represents the suppression of the inherent vowel.

Numerals

Gurmukhi has its own set of numerals that behave exactly as Hindu-Arabic numerals do. These are used extensively in older texts. In modern contexts, they are being replaced by standard Latin numerals although they are still in widespread use.

PUNJABI LITERATURE

Punjabi literature, specifically literary works written in the Punjabi language, is characteristic of the historical Punjab of India and Pakistan and the Punjabi diaspora. The Punjabi language is written in several scripts, of which the Shahmukhi and Gurmukhî scripts are the most commonly used in Pakistan and India, respectively.

Medieval era

The earliest Punjabi literature is found in the fragments of writings of the 11th Nath yogis Gorakshanath and Charpatnah which is primarily spiritual and mystical in tone. Notwithstanding this early yogic literature, the Punjabi literary tradition is popularly seen to commence with Fariduddin Ganjshakar (1173–1266). whose Sufi poetry was compiled after his death in the *Adi Granth*.

Mughal and Sikh periods

The *Janamsakhis*, stories on the life and legend of Guru Nanak (1469–1539), are early examples of Punjabi prose literature. Nanak himself composed Punjabi verse incorporating vocabulary from Sanskrit, Arabic, Persian, and other South Asian languages as characteristic of the Gurbani tradition. Punjabi Sufi poetry developed under Shah Hussain (1538–1599), Sultan Bahu (1628–1691), Shah Sharaf (1640–1724), Ali Haider (1690–1785), Saleh Muhammad Safoori and Bulleh Shah (1680–1757). In contrast to Persian poets, who had preferred the *ghazal* for poetic expression, Punjabi Sufi poets tended to compose in the *Kafi*.

Punjabi Sufi poetry also influenced other Punjabi literary traditions particularly the Punjabi Qissa, a genre of romantic tragedy which also derived inspiration from Indic, Persian and Quranic sources. The Qissa of *Heer Ranjha* by Waris Shah (1706–1798) is among the most popular of Punjabi qisse. Other popular stories include *Sohni Mahiwal* by Fazal Shah, *Mirza Sahiba* by Hafiz Barkhudar (1658–1707), *Sassi Punnun* by Hashim Shah (1735?–1843?), and *Qissa Puran Bhagat* by Qadaryar (1802–1892).

Heroic ballads known as *Vaar* enjoy a rich oral tradition in Punjabi. Prominent examples of heroic or epic poetry include Guru Gobind Singh's in *Chandi di Var* (1666–1708). The semi-historical *Nadir Shah Di Vaar* by Najabat describes the invasion of India by Nadir Shah in 1739. The Jangnama, or 'War Chronicle,' was introduced into Punjabi literature during the

Mughal period; the Punjabi *Jangnama* of Shah Mohammad (1780–1862) recounts the First Anglo-Sikh War of 1845–46.

British Raj era

The Victorian novel, Elizabethan drama, free verse and Modernism entered Punjabi literature through the introduction of British education during the Raj. The first Punjabi printing press (using Gurmukhi font) was established through a Christian mission at Ludhiana in 1835, and the first Punjabi dictionary was published by Reverend J. Newton in 1854.

The Punjabi novel developed through Nanak Singh (1897–1971) and Vir Singh. Starting off as a pamphleteer and as part of the Singh Sabha Movement, Vir Singh wrote historical romance through such novels as Sundari, Satwant Kaur and Baba Naudh Singh, whereas Nanak Singh helped link the novel to the storytelling traditions of Qissa and oral tradition as well as to questions of social reform.

The novels, short stories and poetry of Amrita Pritam (1919–2005) highlighted, among other themes, the experience of women, and the Partition of India. Punjabi poetry during the British Raj moreover began to explore more the experiences of the common man and the poor through the work of Puran Singh (1881–1931). Other poets meanwhile, such as Dhani Ram Chatrik (1876–1957), Diwan Singh (1897–1944) and Ustad Daman (1911–1984), explored and expressed nationalism in their poetry during and after the Indian freedom movement. Chatrik's poetry, steeped in Indian traditions of romance and classical poetry, often celebrated varied moods of nature in his verse as well as feelings of patriotism. Brought up on English and American poetry, Puran Singh was also influenced by Freudian psychology in his oftentimes unabashedly sensuous poetry.

Modernism was also introduced into Punjabi poetry by Prof. Mohan Singh (1905–78) and Shareef Kunjahi. The Punjabi diaspora also began to emerge during the Raj and also produced poetry whose theme was revolt against British rule in *Ghadar di Gunj* (*Echoes of Mutiny*).

Post-Independence

Western Punjab (Pakistan)

Najm Hossein Syed, Fakhar Zaman and Afzal Ahsan Randhawa are some of the more prominent names in West Punjabi literature produced in Pakistan since 1947. Literary criticism in Punjabi has also emerged through the efforts of West Punjabi scholars and poets, Shafqat Tanvir Mirza, Ahmad Salim, and Najm Hosain Syed (b. 1936).

The work of Zaman and Randhawa often treats the rediscovery of Punjabi identity and language in Pakistan since 1947. Ali's short story collection *Kahani Praga* received the Waris Shah Memorial Award in 2005 from the Pakistan Academy of Letters. Mansha Yaad also received the Waris Shah Award for his collection *Wagda Paani* in 1987, and again in 1998 for his novel *Tawan TawaN Tara*, as well as the *Tamgha-e-Imtiaz* (*Pride of Performance*) in 2004. The most critically successful writer in recent times has been Mir Tanha Yousafi who has won the Massod Khaddar Posh Trust Award 4 times, and has had his books transliterated into Gurmukhi for Indian Punjabi readers.

Urdu poets of the Punjab have also written Punjabi poetry including Munir Niazi (1928–2006).

The poet who introduced new trends in Punjabi poetry is Pir Hadi abdul Mannan. Though a Punjabi poet, he also wrote poetry in Urdu.

Eastern Punjab (India)

Amrita Pritam (1919–2005), Jaswant Singh Rahi (1930–1996), Shiv Kumar Batalvi (1936–1973), Surjit Patar (1944–) and Pash (1950–1988) are some of the more prominent poets and writers of East Punjab (India). Pritam's *Sunehe* (*Messages*) received the Sahitya Akademi in 1982. In it, Pritam explores the impact of social morality on women. Kumar's epic *Luna* (a dramatic retelling of the legend of Puran Bhagat) won the Sahitya Akademi Award in 1965. Socialist themes of revolution meanwhile influenced writers like Pash whose work demonstrates the influence of Pablo Neruda and Octavio Paz.

Punjabi fiction in modern times has explored themes in modernist and post-modernist literature. Punjabi culture. Moving from the propagation of Sikh thought and ideology to the themes of the Progressive Movement, the short story in Punjabi was taken up by Nanak Singh, Charan Singh Shaheed, Joshua Fazal Deen, and Heera Singh Dard. Women writers such as Ajit kaur and Daleep Kaur Tiwana meanwhile have questioned cultural patriarchy and the subordination of women in their work. Hardev Grewal has introduced a new genere to Punjabi fiction called Punjabi Murder Mystery in 2012 with his Punjabi novel "Eh Khudkushi Nahin Janab! Qatl Hai" (published by Lahore Books). Kulwant Singh Virk (1921-1987) won the Sahitya Akedemi award for his collection of short stories "Nave Lok" in 1967. His stories are gripping and provide deep insight into the rural and urban modern Punjab. He has been hailed as the "emperor of Punjabi short stories".

Modern Punjab drama developed through Ishwar Nanda's Ibsen-influenced *Suhag* in 1913, and Gursharan Singh who helped popularize the genre through live theatre in Punjabi villages. Sant Singh Sekhon, Kartar Singh Duggal, and Balwant Gargi have written plays, with Atamjit has also been awarded the Sahitya Akademi Award in 2010 for his play *Tatti Tawi De Vich.*

Diaspora Punjabi literature

Punjabi diaspora literature has developed through writers in the United Kingdom, Canada, Australia, and the United States, as well as writers in Africa such as Ajaib Kamal, born in 1932 in Kenya, and Mazhar Tirmazi, writer of famous song "Umraan Langhiyan Pabhan Bhaar." Themes explored by diaspora writers include the cross-cultural experience of Punjabi migrants, racial discrimination, exclusion, and assimilation, the experience of women in the diaspora, and spirituality in the modern world. Second generation writers of Punjabi ancestry such as Rupinderpal Singh Dhillon (writes under the name

Roop Dhillon) have explored the relationship between British Punjabis and their immigrant parents as well as experiment with surrealism, science-fiction and crime-fiction. Bhupinder kaur Sadhaura (1971-)have biography of peer Budhu Shah Ji, book name is Guru Bhagat Peer Budhu Shah (hanoured by Haryana Punjabi Sahitya Academy). Other known writers include Sadhu Binning and Ajmer Rode (Canada), Mazhar Tirmazi, Amarjit Chandan, Avtar Singh Sandhu(Paash) (1950–1988)and Surjit Kalsi. The most successful writer has been Shivcharan Jaggi Kussa.

MODERN LITERATURE

In the literary sphere Punjab's position is secound to none. In poetry the immortal songs of Bhai Vir Singh, Dhani Ram Chatrik, Amrita Pritam, Mohan Singh, Balwant Bawa, Preetam Singh Safeer, Avtar Singh Azad, Prabhjot Kaur and others have a soul moving quality. In thought, expression and universality of appeal Punjabi Poetry today is as rich and asthetic as the poetry of any other language of the country. In the sphere of drama, novel and short story, the path blazed by I.C. Nandha, Nanak Singh and Gurbax Singh had attracted first rate talent in Balwant Gargi, Sheela Bhatia, Gurdial Singh Khosla, Harcharan Singh, Sant Singh Sekhon, Kartar Singh duggal, Kulwant Singh, Navtej and a host of other writers. There is a regular spate of literary output of great merit. The short story seems to have found a rich fertile soil in Punjab, with the result that the Punjabi short story can hold its head high in competition with any regional short story. Even in all India sphere of Hindi, the Punjabi writters like Yashpal, Upinder Nath Ashok, Pt. Sudarshan, Mohan Rakesh, Dev Raj Dinesh, Charanjit, Chandergupt Vidyalankar, Rajiv Pannikar hold top positions. With the devotion of such votaries, the Punjab literature is destined to become one of the richest modern Indian literature in the years to come.

5

Geography and Flora & Fauna

GEOGRAPHY

Punjab is in northwestern India and has a total area of 50,362 square kilometres (19,445 sq mi). Punjab is bounded by Pakistan on the west, Jammu and Kashmir on the north, Himachal Pradesh on the northeast and Haryana and Rajasthan on the south. Most of the Punjab lies in a fertile, alluvial plain with many rivers and an extensive irrigation canal system. A belt of undulating hills extends along the northeastern part of the state at the foot of the Himalayas. Its average elevation is 300 metres (980 ft) above sea level, with a range from 180 metres (590 ft) in the southwest to more than 500 metres (1,600 ft) around the northeast border. The southwest of the state is semiarid, eventually merging into the Thar Desert. The Shiwalik Hills extend along the northeastern part of the state at the foot of the Himalayas.

The soil characteristics are influenced to a limited extent by the topography, vegetation and parent rock. The variation in soil profile characteristics are much more pronounced because of the regional climatic differences. Punjab is divided into three distinct regions on the basis of soil types: southwestern, central, and eastern. Punjab falls under seismic zones II, III, and IV. Zone II is considered a low-damage risk zone; zone III is considered a moderate-damage risk zone; and zone IV is considered a high-damage risk zone.

Most of the Punjab is an alluvial plain, bounded by mountains to the North. Despite its dry conditions, it is a rich agricultural area due to the extensive irrigation made possible by the great river system traversing it. The Indian Punjab is the wealthiest state in the country per capita, with most of the revenue generated from agriculture. Punjab region Summer temperatures can reach 47° C (116.6° F). Punjab region temperature range: -10° to 50° C (MIN/MAX).

Pakistan covers an area of 796,095 sq. km lying between latitude 24 degree and 37 degree North and longitude 62 degree and 75 degree East. The country borders Iran on the west, India in the east, Afghanistan in the north and north-west and the People's Republic of China in the north-west to north-east.

Pakistan is a land of many splendours. The scenery changes northward from coastal beaches, lagoons and mangrove swamps in the south to sandy deserts, desolate plateaus, fertile plains, and dissected upland in the middle and high mountains with beautiful valleys, snow-covered peaks and eternal glaciers in the north. The variety of landscape divides Pakistan into six major regions: the North High Mountainous Region, the Western Low Mountainous Region, the Balochistan Plateau, the Potohar Upland, the Punjab and the Sindh Plains.

Stretching in the north, from east to west, are a series of high mountain ranges, which separate Pakistan from China, Russia and Afghanistan. They include the Himalayas, the Karakoram and Hindukush. With the assemblage of 35 giant peaks over 24,000 ft. (7,315 m) high, the region is the climber's paradise. Many peaks are higher than 26,000 ft. The world's second highest peak K 2 *(the "K" is the initial letter of the name of mountain Karakoram)* tops at 28,250 ft. Inhospitable and technically more difficult to climb than even "Everest" they have taken the biggest toll of human lives in the annals of mountaineering.

This region is home not only to some of the world's highest peaks but also some of the longest glaciers- *huge solidified rivers of ice sliding ponderously down into the valleys where they melt, adding to the flood of the mighty Indus and its tributaries*. Baltoro and Pasu-both over 50 km long, are two famous glaciers. Besides these peaks and glaciers the region abounds in large lakes, and green valleys, which have combined at places to produce beautiful resorts such as Gilgit, Hunza, Chitral, Kaghan and Swat. Due to numerous streams and rivulets, thick forests of pine and junipers, and, a vast variety of fauna and flora, the Chitral, Kaghan and Swat have particularly earned the reputation of being the most enchanting tourist resorts of Pakistan.

The access route to this region is along famous Karakoram Highway. This high way is probably most dramatic road in the world and is an engineering marvel. Stretching 616 km from Thakot, not far north of Islamabad, it climbs 15,072 ft. to the top of the Khunjerab Pass, which marks the border between Pakistan and China. It was built as joint project between the Chinese and Pakistani governments. A great part of it was carved by explosives and bulldozers out of the scree and sheer rock faces of the mountains. For each kilometer laid down, a life was lost in rockfalls and avalanches. Landslides and earth tremors still pose a threat to travellers. Experts from the Pakistan Army's Frontiers Works Organization, the engineering section charged with maintaining the road, predict they will be patching and rebuilding continuously for the next 50 years at least. Nevertheless, it has effectively linked up Pakistan's northern areas with the mainstream of national life. By cutting the journey to the federal capital (Islamabad) from several days to a mere 18 hours it has given a significant boost to regional trade and commerce.

South of the high mountains, the ranges lose their height gradually and settle down finally in the Margalla hills (2,000-3,000 ft.) in the vicinity of Islamabad.

The Western Low Mountain Region spreads from the Swat and Chitral hills in a north-south direction, and covers a large portion of the North-West Frontier Province. North of the river Kabul their altitude ranges from 5,000 to 6,000 ft. in Mohmand and Malakand hills. South of the river Kabul spreads the Koh-e-Sofed Range with a general height of 10,000 ft. Its highest peak, Skaram, being 15,620 ft. South of Koh-e-Sofed are the Kohat and Waziristan hills (5,000 ft.) which are traversed by the Kurram and Tochi rivers, and are bounded on south by Gomal river. South of the Gomal river, the Sulaiman mountains run for a distance of about 483 km in a north-south direction. At 11,295 ft. is the highest peak called Tahkt-e-Sulaiman.

The Western Mountains have a number of passes, which are special geographical and historical interest. For centuries, they have been watching numerous kings, generals and preachers passing through them and the events that followed brought about momentous changes in the annals of mankind. Khyber Pass, the largest and the most renowned of these, is 56 km long and connects Kabul in Afghanistan with the fertile vale of Peshawar in the NWFP. The Tochi pass connects Ghazni in Afghanistan with Bannu in Pakistan and the Gomal Pass provides a route from Afghanistan to Dera Ismail Khan, which overlooks the Punjab Plain. The Bolan Pass connects the Sindh Plain with Quetta in Balochistan and onward through Chaman with Afghanistan.

Balochistan Plateau lies in the East of Sulaiman range. The average altitude is about 2,000 ft. The physical features of the plateau are very varied but mountains, plateaus and basins predominate the scene. The mountains are carved off by innumerable channels and hill torrents, which contain water only after rains. Very little water, however, reaches the basins lying on their foot. Comparatively more important rivers are Zhob, Bolan, and Mulla located in the northeastern portion of Balochistan. Kalat Plateau at 7,000 -8,000 ft., in the centre of Balochistan is the most important plateau.

The largest desert is found in Balochistan. This is an area of inland drainage and dry lakes, the largest of which is Hamume-Mashkhel which is 87 km long and 35 km wide. The surface is littered with sun-cracked clay, oxidized pebbles, salty marshes and crescent-shaped moving sand dunes. The area is known particularly for its constant mirages and sudden sandstorms. Balochistan is rich in mineral wealth of natural gas, coal, chromite, lead, sulphur and marble. The reserves of natural gas at Sui are among the largest in the world. The gas is piped to Karachi, Hyderabad, Sukkur, Multan, Faisalabad, Lahore, Rawalpindi and Quetta for use as industrial power.

The Potohar Upland commonly called the Potohar Plateau, lies to the south of northern mountains and is flanked in the west by River Indus and in the east by River Jhelum. This 1,000-2,000 ft. upland is a typical arid landscape with denuded and broken terrain characterized by undulations and irregularities. These are a few outlying spurs of Salt Range in the south, and those of Khair Murad and Kala Chitta Range in the north. The ramparts of the Salt Range stretching from east to west in the south separate Potohar from the Punjab Plain. The real importance of the Salt Range lies in the large deposits of pure salt at Khewra and Kalabagh and the large seams of coal at Dandot and Makerwal.

The Punjab Plain comprises mainly the province of Punjab. It is the gifted fertile land of River Indus and its five eastern tributaries-Jhelum, Chenab, Ravi, Sutlej and Beas. The plain spreads from the south of Potohar up to Mithankot, where Sulaiman Range approaches river Indus. A unique network of canals extensively irrigates the entire plain. This system has been greatly expanded and improved in recent years by the construction of link-canals, dams, and barrages. Two large dams-Tarbela Dam on river Indus and Mangla Dam on river Jhelum having water storage capacities of 11.1 million acre ft. and 5.55 million acre ft. respectively, have been built. Irrigation is also supplemented by summer and winter rains (15-20 inches) and a variety of crops are produced. The major ones being wheat, rice, cotton, and sugarcane. The region has earned the name of grainary of Pakistan.

Sindh Plain comprises mainly the province of Sindh and stretches between the Punjab Plain and the Arabian Sea. River Indus flows here as a single river. The plain comprises of a vast fertile tract stretching westward from the narrow strip of flood plain on the right bank of River Indus, and a vast expanse of desert stretching eastward from the left bank. It is the heart of the Indus Valley Civilization dating back to 3rd millennium BC. Thousands of tourists from all over the world are attracted every year to visit the ruins of Moenjodaro near Larkana. This area yields abundant crops of rice, wheat and cotton. There are many lakes in Sindh which attracts thousands migratory birds during the winter season from Central Asia. Manchhar lake with its highly pulsating expanse of about 200 sq. miles of area is the largest lake. Further south stretches the Indus Delta, which is a savage waste. At the extreme northwestern end of delta stands Karachi, the largest city and the industrial and commercial hub of Pakistan. It is also a port for Pakistan and terminal of Pakistan's railway system.

DEMOGRAPHICS

Ethnic ancestries of modern Punjabis include Indo-Aryan, and some Indo-Scythian and Indo-Parthian settlers of the region, including Indo-Greek peoples since ancient times; along with native Dravidian. With the advent of Islam, settlers from Persia, Afghanistan and Central Asia have also integrated into Punjabi society. Sikhism is the main religion of the Indian Punjab-it arose in the Punjab itself. About 62% of the population is Sikh, 36% is Hindu, and the rest is Christian and Muslim. Indian Punjab contains the holy Sikh city of Amritsar.

The states of Haryana and Himachal Pradesh, formerly constituents of the British province of Punjab, are mostly Hindu-majority. Most Pakistani & Indian Punjabis largely have Jat ancestry, which is comprised mainly of Sikhs and a number of Hindus. Indian Punjabis speak Punjabi language written in Gurmukhi script. Islam is the religion of more than 98% of the population of the Punjab in Pakistan. There are small Hindu and Sikh minorities among others. Pakistan uses the Shahmukhi script, that is closer to Persian script. In total Pakistan has 70 million Punjabis, and India has 39 million Punjabis.

ETYMOLOGY

The name Punjab means "land of five rivers", and literally translates from Persian into the words *Panj*, cognate with Sanskrit *Panca*, meaning "five", and *Ab* (AE), cognate with Sanskrit *Ap*, meaning "water" respectively. The rivers, tributaries of the Indus River, are the Jhelum, Chenab, Ravi, Sutlej and Beas. The five rivers, now divided between India and Pakistan, merge to form the Panjnad, which joins the Indus.

The first known use of the word Punjab is in the book *Tarikh-e-Sher Shah* (1580), which mentions the construction of a fort by "Sher Khan of Punjab". The name is mentioned again in *Ain-e-Akbari* (part 1), written by Abul Fazal, who also mentions that the territory of Punjab was divided into two provinces, Lahore and Multan. Similarly in the second volume of *Ain-e-Akbari*, the title of a chapter includes the word *Punjab* in it. The Mughal King Jahangir also mentions the word *Punjab* in *Tuzk-i-Janhageeri*.

DISTRICTS

Punjab state is divided into 20 administrative districts (listed below):

1. Amritsar District
2. Barnala
3. Bathinda District
4. Firozpur District
5. Fatehgarh Sahib District
6. Faridkot District
7. Gurdaspur District
8. Hoshiarpur District
9. Jalandhar District
10. Kapurthala District

11. Ludhiana District
12. Mansa District
13. Moga District
14. Mohali District
15. Muktsar District
16. Nawanshahr District
17. Patiala District
18. Rupnagar District
19. Sangrur District
20. Tarn Taran District

REGION

Punjab is a region straddling the border between India and Pakistan. Punjab has a long history and rich cultural heritage. The people of the Punjab are called Punjabis and they speak a language called Punjabi. The main religions in Indian Punjab are Sikhism and Hinduism, while Islam is the majority in Pakistani Punjab.

Ancient Punjab (or the Greater Punjab) had comprised vast territories of Northern India, eastern Pakistan and parts of Afghanistan. It once extended as far as river Yamuna in the east. The Panjabis, *i.e.*, the inhabitants of Panjab, in ancient times, were also known as Vahikas or Arattas. The name comprised such ethnic elements as the Gandharas, Prasthalas, Khasas, Vasatis, Trigartas, Pauravas, Malavas, Yaudheyas, Saindhavas, Sauviras; the Iranian and trans-frontier peoples such as the Kambojas, Pahlavas; and the Persianised Ionians (Yavanas) as well as the nomadic Scythians, also called Shakas.

The region, populated by Indo-Aryans, has been ruled by many different empires and ethnic groups, including the ancient Greeks, Persians, Arabs, Turks, Mughals, Afghans, Sikhs and British. Subsequently, after 1947, it was partitioned between India and Pakistan.

A historical region of the northwest Indian sub-continent bounded by the Indus and Yamuna rivers. It was a centre of the prehistoric Indus Valley civilization and after c. 1500 B.C.

the site of early Aryan settlements. The advent of Islam during the eighth century brought the region into prominence, and under the Mughals, Punjab came to light as the cultural heart of the sub-continent. The Sikh rebellion and capture of the region accelerated this development until the region was annexed by Britain. It was subsequently partitioned between India and Pakistan in 1947.

Once a single entity, it is now split between two nations: Pakistani Punjab, which comprises the majority of the region and Indian Punjab, which has been further sub-divided into north-western Indian Punjab, Haryana, Himachal Pradesh and Delhi. The Pakistani part of the region covers an area of 205,344 square kilometres, (79,284 square miles), whereas the Indian section is 50,362 square kilometres (19,445 square miles).

The populations of the region are similarly divided as 86,084,000 (2005) in West Punjab (Pakistan) and 24,289,296 (2000) in East Punjab (India). Punjabi is spoken by (approx) 90% of population in Pakistani Punjab and 92.2% in Indian Punjab. The capital city of undivided Punjab was Lahore, which now sits close to the partition line as the capital of West Punjab. Indian Punjab has as its capital, the city of Chandigarh. With partition, Indian Punjab now uses the Gurmukhi script, while West Punjab maintains the Shahmukhi script.

CLIMATE

The geography and subtropical latitudinal location of Punjab lead to large variations in temperature from month to month. Even though only limited regions experience temperatures below 0 °C (32 °F), ground frost is commonly found in the majority of Punjab during the winter season. The temperature rises gradually with high humidity and overcast skies. However, the rise in temperature is steep when the sky is clear and humidity is low.

The maximum temperatures usually occur in mid-May and June. The temperature remains above 40 °C (104 °F) in the entire region during this period. Ludhiana recorded the highest maximum temperature at 46.1 °C (115.0 °F) with Patiala and

Amritsar recording 45.5 °C (113.9 °F). The maximum temperature during the summer in Ludhiana remains above 41 °C (106 °F) for a duration of one and a half months. These areas experience the lowest temperatures in January. The sun rays are oblique during these months and the cold winds control the temperature at daytime.

Agricultural fields of Punjab during the monsoon

Punjab experiences its minimum temperature from December to February. The lowest temperature was recorded at Amritsar (0.2 °C (32.4 °F)) and Ludhiana stood second with 0.5 °C (32.9 °F). The minimum temperature of the region remains below 5 °C (41 °F) for almost two months during the winter season. The highest minimum temperature of these regions in June is more than the daytime maximum temperatures experienced in January and February. Ludhiana experiences minimum temperatures above 27 °C (81 °F) for more than two months. The annual average temperature in the entire state is approximately 21 °C (70 °F). Further, the mean monthly temperature range varies between 9 °C (48 °F) in July to approximately 18 °C (64 °F) in November.

Seasons

Punjab experiences three main seasons. They are:

- Hot Season (mid-April to the end of June)
- Rainy Season (early July to the end of September)
- Cold Season (early December to the end of February).

Apart from these three, the state experiences transitional seasons like:

- Pre-summer season (March to mid-April): This is the period of transition between winter and summer.
- Post-monsoon season (September to end of November): This is the period of transition between monsoon and winter seasons.

Summer

Punjab starts experiencing mildly hot temperatures in February. However, the actual summer season commences in mid-April. The area experiences pressure variations during the summer months. The atmospheric pressure of the region remains around 987 millibar during February and it reaches 970 millibar in June.

Rainy season

The monsoon brings joy to the agricultural sector as farmers become very busy. Punjab's rainy season begins in first week of July as monsoon currents generated in the Bay of Bengal bring rain to the region.

Winter

Temperature variation is minimal in January. The mean night and day temperatures fall to 5 °C (41 °F) and 12 °C (54 °F), respectively.

Post-Monsoon transitional season

The monsoon begins to reduce by the second week of September. This brings a gradual change in climate and temperature. The time between October and November is the transitional period between monsoon and winter seasons. Weather during this period is generally fair and dry.

Post-Winter transitional season

The effects of winter diminish by the first week of March. The hot summer season commences in mid-April. This period is marked by occasional showers with hail storms and squalls that cause extensive damage to crops. The winds remain dry and warm during the last week of March, commencing the harvest period.

Rainfall

- Monsoon Rainfall: Monsoon season provides most of the rainfall for the region. Punjab receives rainfall from the monsoon current of the Bay of Bengal. This monsoon current enters the state from the southeast in the first week of July.
- Winter Rainfall: The winter season remains very cool with temperatures falling below freezing at some places. Winter also brings in some western disturbances. Rainfall in the winter provides relief to the farmers as some of the winter crops in the region of Shivalik Hills are entirely dependent on this rainfall. As per meteorological statistics, the sub-Shivalik area receives more than 100 millimetres (3.9 in) of rainfall in the winter months.

GEOGRAPHIC DISTRIBUTION

Punjabis in Pakistan: The Punjabis found in Pakistan are composed of clans and tribes (the aforementioned *qaums*) often with a correspondence with traditional occupations. Pre-Islamic Kambohs, Gujjars, Jats and Rajputs (such as the Janjuas), predominate with the Gakhars, Awans, and Arains, comprising the main tribes in the north, while Gilanis, Gardezis, Quraishi are found in the south. Hence Punjabis in Pakistan especially in major urban cities have diverse origins with many post Islamic settlers tracing their origin to Afghanistan, Persia,

Arabia, Kashmir and Central Asia. Punjabis have been traditionally farmers and warriors which has transferred into modern times with a dominance of agriculture and the military in Pakistan.

In addition, Punjabis in Pakistan have been quite prominent politically having had many elected Members of Parliament. As the most ardent supporters of a Pakistani state, the Punjabis in Pakistan have shown a strong pre-dilection towards the adoption of Urdu, while still identifying themselves as ethnic Punjabis for the most part. Religious homogeniety remains elusive as a Sunni-Shia divide and a Christian minority have not completely wiped out diversity since the partition of British India. A variety of related sub-groups exist in Pakistan and are often considered by many Pakistani Punjabis to be simply regional Punjabis including the Seraikis (who overlap and are often considered transitional with the Sindhis) and Punjabi Pathans (which publications like *Encyclopaedia Britannica* consider a transitional group between Punjabis and Pathans). Punjabis of India Indian Punjabis tend to correspond to various caste criteria with the Sikhs showing more unity overall, while Hindu Punjabis sometimes remain stratified along caste lines. Some of the major subgroups of the Punjabis in India include: Ahirs, Aroras, Banias, Bhatias, Brahmins, Dalits, Gujjars, Jats, Kalals/Ahluwalias, Kambojs, Khatris, Labanas, Rajputs, Sainis, Sansis, Soods and Tarkhans/Ramgarhias. Most of these subgroups can be further sub-divided into clans and family groups.

The Punjabi Sikh community remains the most prominent proponents of a Punjabi ethnic identity in India, while many Hindu Punjabis have shown a similar linguistic and cultural shift that corresponds with the Punjabis in Pakistan, as the identification of Hindi as a mother tongue rather than Punjabi has become more pronounced following political conflict between Sikhs and Hindus that devolved into serious violence in the 1980s and early 1990s. However, most Hindu Punjabis do not claim this to be true, and still maintain a strong Punjabi heritage.

Most of East Punjab's (today's Punjab, Haryana, Himachal Pradesh, Delhi and Chandigarh) Muslims left for West Punjab in 1947. However, a small community still survives today, mainly in Malerkotla, the only Muslim princely state among the seven that formed the erstwhile Patiala and East Punjab States Union (PEPSU). The other six (mostly Sikh) states were: Patiala, Nabha, Jind, Faridkot, Kapurthala and Kalsia.

The Punjab region within India maintains a strong influence on the culture of India and the perceived culture of India towards the rest of the world. Numerous Bollywood film productions use the Punjabi language within its songs and dialogues as well as traditional dances and instruments such as the bhangra and tabla. Prime Ministers of India including Gulzarilal Nanda and Inder Kumar Gujral in the past, and Dr. Manmohan Singh, at present, are Punjabis, as are numerous players in the Indian cricket team (both past and present including Harbhajan Singh, Bishen Singh Bedi, Kapil Dev, Yuvraj Singh, etc.).

The Punjabi Diaspora: The Punjabi people have emigrated in large numbers to many parts of the world. The United Kingdom has a significant number of Punjabis from both India and Pakistan as does Canada and the United States. The Middle East has a large immigrant community of Punjabis, in places such as the UAE and Kuwait. There are large communities in East Africa including the countries of Kenya, Uganda and Tanzania. Punjabis have also emigrated to Australia, New Zealand and Southeast Asia including Malaysia, Thailand, Singapore and Hong Kong.

LAND

The word "Punjab" is made up of two Persian words 'Panj' and 'Aab'. Panj means five and Aab means water. This name was probably given to this land possibly in an era when this region came into close contact with Persia. The Punjab was known as land of five rivers because of the five rivers that ran through it. They are Indus, Ravi, Beas, Sutlaj and Ghaggar. Prior to Persian period this region was known by different names at different times. Probably, at the height of its glory it was known as Sapta Sindhu, land of the seven rivers, namely Sindhu (Indus), Vitasta (Jehlum), Asuhi (chenab), Purshin (Ravi), Vipasa (Beas), Satadru (Sutleg) and Saruri (Saraswati). The last one is a dried up stream now and its traces are found in the present seasonal streams that flow near Pehowa in Haryana. During Greek occupation, the territory had shrunk into the area covering the five rivers.

In 1947 when India was partitioned, the larger half of Punjab went to Pakistan. In 1966 the Indian smaller half was further divided into three: Punjab, Haryana and Himachal Pradesh.

According to 1991 census, its population came to 20.19 million. Punjab, thus represents about 1.6 percent of the area and 2.39 percent of the population of the country. The latitudinal and longitudinal extends the Punjab are from 29° 32' to 32° 32'N and 73° 55' to 76° 50'E. Punjab is bounded on the west by Pakistan, on the North by Jammu and Kashmir, on the north east by Himachal Pradesh and on the south by Haryana and Rajasthan.

Physically, the state may be divided into two parts; sub-Shivalik Strip and Sutlebj- Ghaggar Plain. The Sub Shivalik strip covers the upper portion of Ropar, Hoshiarpur and Gurdaspur districts. The Sutlej- Ghaggar plain embraces the other districts of the Punjab. For administrative purposes it is divided into three division and 45 sub-division. There are 12,342 villages and 134 towns in the state.

Physical Features

From the geographical and physiographic point of view, Punjab falls into two regions: the Shivaliks and the Plain.

The Shivalik

This region covers the outer range of the Shivalik Hills and is approximately 6 to 10 kms in width. Their height ranges between 400 and 700 metres above sea level. It consists of conglomerates, clays and silts-all having the character of fluviatile deposits of rivers and stream.

The origin of the Shivalik Hills has been explained differently by different geologists. One view advanced is that the present Shivalik Range is the flood plain of a big river to whom pilgrims gave the name Indo-Brahm and Pascoe- Shivalik. According to another view the basin of deposition was a continuous lagoon or fore-deep formed in front of the Himalayan Range.

The low range of the Shivalik Hills separates the Himalayas from the plains. The Shivalik region covers the eastern most areas of Ropar, Hoshiarpur and Gudaspur districts and runs like a wall, north-west to south-east, separating the Sirsa and Una valleys of Himachal Pradesh from the plain areas towards the west.

The Plains

The Punjab plain is a part of the great Indo-Gangetic plain which is a synclinal basin formed by the elevation of the Himalayas. One group of geologists hold this area to be afore-deep formed in front of the stable peninsular India at a time when the Tethyan Sediments were thrust southwards and compressed against that stable block. Another group assumes the Indo-Gangetic plain to be the site of a rift valley. The rivers of the region indicate that the plain is the result of recent deposition and these very rivers have formed the plain.

The Punjab plain lies between 180 and 300 meters above sea level. It is higher near the Shivalik Hills but slopes away from them. The tract covering central Punjab ranges between 230 and 270 metres above sea level while western Bhatinda and Ferozepur districts lie below 230 metres above sea level. The land slopes from east to west. The gradient is much more in the east than in the west.

The work of the two important agents of mechanical weathering, wind and running water, is well exemplified in this area. The action of wind in the western side and the action of running water near the Shivalik Range have modified the face of this region to impart to the different tracts a contrasting look.

Climate

The sum total of weather over a period constitutes the climate. It is the net result of various factors, the most important of which are temperature, precipitation, wind, sunshine and clouds. Climate has a profound effect on the economic development of a region. It has also a great bearing on the social and cultural activities of the people.

Seasons

There are three well defined seasons in the Punjab. These are:

1. Hot Season (mid-April to the end of June)
2. Rainy Season (early July to the end of September)
3. Cold Season (early December to the end of February)

The transitional seasons are:

1. Post-monsoon (September to end of November). It is transitional period between the rainy and cold seasons.
2. Pre-hot season (March to mid-April). It is a transitional period between the cold and hot seasons.

Hot Season

The temperature begins to rise from February onwards. Though the real hot seasons starts in mid-April, the rising temperature breaks the high pressure belt in the north-west of the Indian peninsula. The atmospheric pressure over this region in February is about 987 milli bars. The minimum is reached in early June when it is near about 970 milli bars.

Rainy Season

This is the most welcome season and the agricultural year starts with its advent. Monsoon winds reach the region normally in the first weeks of July. The Bay of Bengal branch of the monsoon current is the main source of rainfall.

Winter Season

The fall in temperature is minimum in January, when the

mean temperature falls to 12°C during day time and to 5°C during the night. The winter season, cherished by the affluent, becomes a curse for the poor who cannot afford warm clothing.

Post-Monsoon Transitional Season

Monsoon normally retreat by the middle of September. With this a gradual change in weather takes place and continuous so till the end of November. Thus October and November are the months with transitional climates between rainy and winter seasons. The weather remains generally dry and fair.

Post-Winter Transitional Season

By early March the winter season begins to fade and by the middle of April, it ultimately emerges as hot season. At times there may be a shower or two accompanied by hail storms and squalls which do a lot of damage to crops. The winds are warm and dry during the last days of March, it is the time for harvest.

Temperature

The sub-tropical latitudinal and continental location of Punjab makes the variation of temperature from month to month very high. Though the minimum air temperature rarely drops below 0° C, ground frost is a common phenomenon in mid -winter. The rise in temperature is gradual when the air has high moisture content with the sky remaining overcast; the rise is however steep when the sky is clear and there is little moisture content in the air.

The highest day time temperature is recorded during the months of May and June. It is 40.4° C at Patiala, 40.4° C at Amristar and 41.2° C at Ludhiana. At Ludhiana the highest maximum temperature on record was 46.1° C while at Amritsar and Patiala the highest record was 45.5° C. The daily maximum temperature at Ludhiana remains above 41° C for 45 days in a year. The lowest maximum temperature is recorded during the month of January. When the sun's rays are more oblique as compared to the other months. The cold winds check the rise of day temperature.

The minimum temperature is lowest from December to February. The lowest minimum temperature recorded at Amristar is 0.2° C and at Ludhiana 0.5°C. At Amristar the minimum temperature remain below 5°C for 55 days. The maximum number of days with the lowest night time temperature are in the month of January. The highest minimum temperature is recorded in the month of June. When it is even higher than the day temperature of December and January. At Ludhiana for 55 days in the year the minimum temperature is as high as 27° C. The maximum number of days with such high night temperature are in the month of June. The annual range of temperature all over the state is around 21°C. The mean monthly range of temperature varies from 9°C in July to about 18°C in November.

Rainfall

The amount of rainfall in the Punjab ranges between 250 mm and 1000 mm. The maximum falling near the Shivalik Hills and the minimum towards the desert in the west. 70 to 80 percent of the total rainfall is concentrated during the three months of south-west monsoon winds and the rest comes during the winter months. There is wide difference in the amount of rainfall experienced in east and west Punjab. Near the hills rainfall is over 1000 mm. Gurdaspur, Hoshiarpur, Ropar district and eastern parts of Patiala receive an annual rainfall of more than 750 mm. The 500 mm rainfall line runs in a north-west to south-east direction and cuts the Punjab into almost two equal zones. The Fazilka tehsil in the extreme west receive a rainfall of less than 250 mm.

Monsoon Rainfall

The major part of annual rainfall is experienced during the monsoon period, when the monsoon current in the Bay of Bengal enters from the south-east. The normal onset of the monsoon in Punjab is in the first week of July.

Winter Rainfall

During the winter season, weather in Punjab is normally cool and dry. This type of weather is associated with the passage of western disturbances through the region.

The importance of winter rainfall in Punjab is immense primarily because of its time and effectiveness. In the area adjoining the Shivalik Hills, winter crops is dependent upon this rainfall. The sub-Shivalik region receives more than 100 mm of rainfall from December to March.

SOIL

Soil is the end product of the parent material resulting from the consistent influence of climate, topography and the natural vegetation over a long period of time. In Punjab the soil characteristics are influenced to a very limited extent by the topography, vegetation and parent rock. The variation in soil profile characteristics are much more pronounced because of the regional climatic differences.

Punjab can be divided into three distinct regions on the basis of soil types.

1. *South-western Punjab:* This region covers the tehsils of Fazilka, Muktsar, Bhatinda, Mansa and parts of Ferozepur which border Haryana and Rajasthan states in the south-west. The soil is predominantly calcareous, developed under hot and arid to semi-arid conditions. The pH value ranges from 7.8 to 8.5 which shows that the soil is normal in reaction. Grey and red desert, calsisol, regosol and alluvial soils are found in this zone. The soil of south-western Punjab can further be sub-divided into two categories.
    (a) *Desert Soil:* The soil covers Fazilka tehsil of Ferozepur district and south-western fringes of Muktsar tehsil of Faridkot district. The soil is deficient in nitrogen, phosphorous and potassium. Wind erosion is a serious problem specially during the hot summer.
    (b) *Sierozem Soil:* This soil is found in Bhatinda district and Faridkot and Muktsar tehsils of Faridkot and most parts of Ferozepur tehsil. The texture of the soil

is sandy loan to silt. The soil is deficient in nitrogen, phosphorous and potash. In some irrigated tracts, alkalinity and salinity pose a problem. Wind erosion is again a serious matter in areas where this soil group is predominant.

2. *Central Punjab:* The soil of this zone has developed under semi-arid condition. The soil is sandy loam to clayey with normal reaction (pH from 7.8 to 8.5). The soil covers the districts of Sangrur, Patiala, Ludhiana, Jalandhar, Kapurthala, Amristar, parts of Gurdaspur, Ferozepur and fringes of Kharar tehsil of Ropar district. Problem of alkalinity and Salinity is quite accute, especially in districts of Amristar, Sangrur, Ferozepur, Gurdaspur and Patiala. The soil of the central zone, generally recognised as alluvial, falls into tow categories.

   (a) *Arid and Brown Soil:* This soil is found in Amristar district (except in the north-eastern half of the Amristar tehsil) in most of Sutlanpur tehsil of Kapurthala, Zira and northern parts of Ferozepur, Moga, Rampur tehsil of Bhatinda, Barnala, Sangrur and Sunam tehsils of Sangrur district and Samana tehsil of Patiala district. The texture is sandy-loam and the fertility is from medium to high. The soil is calcareous and lacks nitrogen but contains a fair amount of phosphorous and potash.

   (b) *Tropical Arid Brown Soil:* This soil covers parts of Amristar, the south-western half of Gurdaspur tehsil, Batala tehsil, Kapurthala district except Sultanpur, Jalandhar, Ludhiana, Patiala and the Malerkotla tehsil of Sangrur district. Some parts in the south-west of Ropar district also fall in the zone. The soil is deficient in nitrogen, potash and phosphorus.

   Water-logging, alkalinity and salinity pose serious problems. The texture of the soil is sandy loam in south-western half and in the flood plains of the rivers but in the north-western half the texture becomes clayey. The fertility of the soil varies from medium to high.

3. *Eastern Punjab:* The soil has developed in the sub-humid foothill areas bordering Himachal Pradesh covering eastern parts of Gurdaspur, Hoshiarpur, Ropar and north-eastern fringes of Patiala district. Because of the undulating topography and fair amount of rainfall, normal erosion is quite common. The fertility of the soil is medium to low and the texture is loamy to clayey. Two soil types are recognised in the zone.

   (a) *Grey Brown Podzolic Soil:* This soil is found in the Pathankot tehsil of Gurdaspur and north-eastern parts of Ropar and Kharar tehsils. Because of surface run-off, the soil is not influenced by leaching, hence profile development is poor. Since the rainfall is heavy, gully erosion is a serious problem. Acidity is from medium to high. The Soil lacks in phosphorous, calcium and zinc. Phosphorus fixation in the soil is high.

   (b) *Reddish Chestnut Soil:* The soil is found in a region covering Hoshiarpur, Ropar and some parts of Gurdaspur tehsils. The carbonates are leached down to the lower layers. The soil is moderately acidic and neutral in reaction (pH 6.5 to 7.5) and is deficient in nitrogen and phosphorus. However, it is free of any accumulation of salt and calcium carbonate.

FLORA AND FAUNA

The plains of Punjab do not have any thick forests. The only available flora are patches of grass, small bushes, and shrubs. In the southeastern part of Punjab and the areas of Gurdaspur, Hoshiarpur and Multan, mangoes are grown. Other varieties of fruit grown in abundance are oranges, apples, figs, quinces, almonds, pomegranates, peaches, mulberries, apricots and plums.

Major cultivation of rich flora and fauna can be seen in the Shivalik ranges. Due its rich flora and fauna, it has been termed a micro-endemiczone of India. There is a wide variety of angiosperms in the area, including 355 types of herbs, 70 types of trees, 70 types of shrubs of all sizes, 19 types of climbers, and 21 types of twines. Besides angiosperms, the region is home to 31 kinds of pteridophytes and 27 kinds of bryophytes, while a special species of gymnosperm named Pinus roxburghii can be seen in the ranges of Punjab.

Agriculture in Punjab

The fauna of the area is rich, with 396 types of birds, 214 kinds of Lepidoptera, 55 varieties of fish, 20 types of reptiles, and 19 kinds of mammals. The state of Punjab has large wetland areas, bird sanctuaries that house numerous species of birds, and many zoological parks. Wetlands include the national wetland Hari-Ke-Pattan, the wetland of Kanjli, and the wetlands of Kapurthala Sutlej. Wildlife sanctuaries include the Harike in the district of Tarn Taran Sahib, the Zoological Park in Rupnagar, Chhatbir Bansar Garden in Sangrur, Aam Khas Bagh in Sirhind, Amritsar's famous Ram Bagh, Shalimar Garden in Kapurthala, and the famous Baradari Garden in the city of Patiala.

Animals and birds

A few of the rivers in Punjab have dangerous species of crocodiles. The extraction of silk from silkworms is another industry that flourishes in the state. Production of bee honey is done in some parts of Punjab. The southern plains are desert land; hence, camels can be seen. Buffaloes graze around the banks of rivers. The northeastern part is home to animals like horses. Wildlife sanctuaries have many more species of wild animals like the otter, wild boar, wildcat, fruit bat, hog deer, flying fox, squirrel and mongoose. Naturally formed forests can be seen in the Shivalik ranges in the districts of Ropar, Gurdaspur and Hoshiarpur. Patiala is home to the Bir forest while the wetlands area in Punjab is home to the famous Mand forest.

Botanical gardens exist throughout Punjab. There is a zoological park and a tiger safari park, as well as three parks dedicated to deer.

The state bird is the baz (northern goshawk). (*Melierax poliopterus*), the state animal is the blackbuck (*Antilope cervicapra*), and the state tree is the shisham (*Dalbergia sissoo*).

FLORA AND FAUNA OF PUNJAB

The plains in the state of Punjab do not have any thick forests, the only available patches are of grass, small bush and shrubs. In the southern east part of state of Punjab and the areas of Hoshiarpur and Multan, the delicious mango fruit is grown. The other varieties of fruits that are grown in abundance here are orange, apple, fig, quince, almond, pomegranate, peach, mulberry, apricot and plum. The region that has major cultivation of rich flora and fauna can be majorly seen in the Shivalik ranges in the state of Punjab. Due to rich flora and fauna in the Shivalik region, it has been also termed as the zone of micro-endemic in India. The variety of angiosperms in the area includes 355 different types of herbs, trees of 70 different types; shrubs all in big and small sizes are of 70 different kinds, climbers of 19 different types can also be seen while 21 different types of twines can also be seen here. Other than angiosperms, other varieties available are 31 kinds of pteridophytes, bryophytes of 27 different kinds while a special species of gymnosperms named as Pinus Roxburghii can be seen in the ranges in state of Punjab. The fauna of the area is also rich that has birds of 396 different types, Lepidoptera is of 214 different kinds, 55 varieties of fish species can also be seen, reptiles of 20 different types are also available and mammals of 19 different kinds can be seen in these ranges. The state of Punjab is adored with large wetland area, number of bird sanctuaries that houses different varieties of numerous species of birds and a large number of zoological parks. Few of them to be named are wetland named as National wetland Hari-Ke-Pattan, the wetland of Kanjli, the wetlands of Kapurthala Sutlej, the number of wildlife sanctuaries include the Harika wildlife in district of Tarn Taran Sahib, Zoological Park in Ropar, Chhatbir Bansar Garden located in Sangrur Aam Khas Bagh situated in Sirhind, Amritsar's famous Ram Bagh, Shalimar Garden in Kapurthala and the famous Baradari Garden in city of Patiala.

Animals and Birds in Punjab

Few of the local rivers in Punjab also have the dangerous species of Crocodiles. The extraction of silk from silkworms is also another industry that flourishes in the state. Production of bee honey is also done in some parts of Punjab. The southern plains in Punjab is desert land hence camel can also be seen. Buffaloes can be seen grazing around the banks of river. The north eastern part has animals like horses. The desert area also has dangerous species of snakes like cobra and sangehur. The wild life sanctuaries have species of wild animals like otter, wild boar, wildcat, fruit bat, hog deer, flying fox, squirrel and mongoose.

Baaz also known as the Eastern Goshawk and Blackbuck known as Antilope cervicapra are the state bird and state animal of Punjab respectively. The Shisham known as Dalbergia Sissoo is the state tree of state of Punjab.

The natural formed forests can be seen in the Shivalik ranges of Punjab area in the districts like Ropar, Gurdaspur and Hoshiarpur. Patiala has the Bir forest while wetlands area in state of Punjab has the famous Mand forest.

There are a number of botanical gardens spread in various areas of Punjab. There is also a zoological park and a tiger safari park. There are a total of 3 parks dedicated to deer.

Agriculture in Punjab

Punjab is a land of agriculture. There are number of medical plants spread in the entire state. Many self driven business of pickle, juices of amla, shivlingi, lassora, hara etc are operated by local women.

Medicine in Punjab

The other industry that is popular in the state of Punjab is processing raw materials to produce medicines and herbal products into an end product like pills, capsules, tea and creams etc. that are further sent for sale in the entire country to various health stores, medical shops and at pharmacists. The herbal products made prepared using leaves, roots, seeds, flowers, fruits, stem etc to produce the end products like tea, lotions, powder, tinctures etc.

6

Economy

INTRODUCTION

Punjab's GDP is 3.17 lakh crore (US$47 billion). Punjab is one of the most fertile regions in India. The region is ideal for wheat-growing. Rice, sugar cane, fruits and vegetables are also grown. Indian Punjab is called the "Granary of India" or "India's bread-basket". It produces 10.26% of India's cotton, 19.5% of India's wheat, and 11% of India's rice. The Firozpur and Fazilka Districts are the largest producers of wheat and rice in the state. In worldwide terms, Indian Punjab produces 2% of the world's cotton, 2% of its wheat and 1% of its rice.

The largest cultivated crop is wheat. Other important crops are rice, cotton, sugarcane, pearl millet, maize, barley and fruit. Rice and wheat are doublecropped in Punjab with rice stalks being burned off over millions of acres prior to the planting of wheat. This widespread practice is polluting and wasteful.

In Punjab the consumption of fertiliser per hectare is 223.46 kg as compared to 90 kg nationally. The state has been awarded the National Productivity Award for agriculture extension services for ten years, from 1991–92 to 1998–99 and from 2001 to 2003–04. In recent years a drop in productivity has been observed, mainly due to falling fertility of the soil. This is believed to be due to excessive use of fertilisers and pesticides over the years. Another worry is the rapidly falling water table on which almost 90% of the agriculture depends; alarming drops have been witnessed in recent years. By some estimates, groundwater is falling by a meter or more per year.

Burning of rice residues after harvest to quickly prepare the land for wheat planting, around Sangrur, Punjab

According to the India State Hunger Index, Punjab has the lowest level of hunger in India.

AGRICULTURE

The principal crops of the state are barley, wheat, paddy, maize and sugarcane. Among the fodder crops are Bajra and Jowar. The green fodder, is very popular with the farmers for feeding milch cattle. Main sources of irrigation are canales and tube wells.

The economy of the state depends primarily upon agriculture. There are two main harvests in the year. Rabi (hari) and Kharif (Sawani). The rabi or spring harvest consists of wheat, gram, barley and some oil seeds, fodder crops, potatoes and winter vegetables. The Kharif or autumn harvest consists of rice, maize, sugarcane, cotton, pulses other than gram and peas, bajra, jowar and vegetables like chillies, onions and gourd. Two system of cropping are in vogue in the state namely Dofasli Harsala and Ekjasli Harsala. The Dofasli Harsala means two harvests in a period of twelve months. Ekfasli Harsala means a single crop in a year.

Historically, Punjab (the five rivers region) has been one of the most fertile regions on earth. The region is ideal for wheat-growing. Rice, sugar cane, fruits and vegetables are also grown. Indian Punjab is called the "Granary of India" or "India's bread-basket." It produces 60% of India's wheat, and 40% of India's rice. In worldwide terms, this represents 1/30th or 3% of the world's production of these crops, so Indian Punjab produces 2% of the world's cotton, 2% of its wheat and 1% of the world's rice. The largest grown crop is wheat. Other important crops are rice, cotton, sugarcane, millet, maize, barley and fruit.

Power

The amount of power consumed in a country is an index of its technological development. The progress of all sector of the economy is proportional to the availability of power. Hydro-electric power is the main source on which most nations depend. Hydro-electric power is needed for turning the wheels of industries, for transportation, for carrying on agricultural operations and for keeping the hearths and homes warm.

Power Availability

Thirty-seven percent of the power came from the common pool projects and the rest from its own projects. About 27 percent of the total energy of the state is provided by the Ropar Thermal Plant while the Bhakra Nangal complex provided 20.3 percent of the total power for the state and the Guru Nanak Thermal plant at Bhatinda accounts for about 21 percent of the energy to the state. Other important sources of power are the Dehar Power plant (13 percent), Shanan Power house at Joginder Nagar (5 percent), Pong Power project (4percent) and UBDC power houses (2 percent).

The common pool projects are the Bhakra Nangal Complex, the Dehar Power plant and the Pong Power plant. Punjab shares about 51 percent of the Power generated from the Bhakra Nangal Complex. 48 percent from the Power generated at the Pong Project.

a. *Bhakra Nangal Complex:* The Bhakra Nangal project is the most prestigious hydro-electric project of India which harnesses the waters of river Sutlej. The Bhakra Nangal project not only provides electric power to Punjab, Haryana and Rajasthan but also to common pool consumers like the Nangal fertilizer factory, the Delhi Electric Supply undertaking, to Himachal Pradesh and to Jammu and Kashmir.
b. *The Upper Bari Doab Canal System (UBDC):* Constructed on River Ravi, north of Pathankot, is the second source of hydroelectricity for the state.
c. *The Shanan Power House:* This power house is installed on River Ohel and is situated at Joginder Nagar in Himachal Pradesh.

Thermal Electricity

In Punjab there are two big thermal plants:

a. *Guru Nanak Thermal Plant:* It was completed in 1974. The Guru Nanak Thermal plant has four units of 440 MW capacity. This is one of the most efficiently run thermal plants in the country.
b. *Ropar Thermal Plant*: The Ropar Thermal project is located at a distance of 11 kilometers from the Ropar-Nagal highway. This project consists of two units capable of generating 210 MW each. The plant is spread over an area of about 2,500 acres on the banks of River Sutlej.

BUSINESS AND INFRASTRUCTURE

Punjab has the best infrastructure in all of India and as result it is becoming enormously attractive to foreign companies looking for bases and manufacturing zones for their Indian operations. The Indian National Council of Applied Economic

Research (NCAER) has ranked Punjab's infrastructure as the best in India. Its road, rail, air and transport system is rated best in the country with ranking of 210 points compared to the national average of 100 in NCAER's infrastructure index. It has highest per capita generation of electricity in India, which is 2.5 times the national average. All major Punjabi cities hugely benefit from this and having one of lowest tariff's in India, including all of Punjab's villages, which have been electrified and connected to the Punjabi electrical power grid since 1974.

- Total Road network 47,605 km
- All cities connected by National Highways.
- All major towns of adjoining states connected by National Highways.
- Percentage of villages connected by metalled roads 97%
- National Highways: 1000 km
- State Highways: 2166 km
- Major Distt. Roads: 1799 km
- Other District Roads: 3340 km
- Link Roads: 31657 km

Source: NCAER & Punjab Government

MACRO-ECONOMIC TREND

This is a chart of trend of gross state domestic product of Punjab at market prices estimated by *Ministry of Statistics and Programme Implementation* with figures in millions of Indian Rupees. The traditional long-term financial policy of the central government is to reward well-performing States.

Year	*Gross State Domestic Product*
1980	50,250
1985	95,060
1990	188,830
1995	386,150
2000	660,100

Punjab's gross state domestic product for 2004 is estimated at $27 billion in current prices.

About 1% of the *S&P CNX 500* conglomerates have corporate offices in Punjab. This is a list of NSE-indexed conglomerates with corporate offices in Punjab. Figures are given in millions of Indian Rupees for 2005.

Rank	*Conglomerate*	*Gross Income*
1	Mahavir Spinning Mills	19,376
2	Punjab Tractors	10,245
3	Abhishek Industries	7,537
4	Nahar Spinning Mills	4,687
5	Nahar Exports	4,293
6	Vardhman Polytex	2,955

INDUSTRIES

Punjab has essentially an agrarian economy with a low industrial output. The absence of basic minerals is the main reason for low level of industrial progress. A notable feature of the industrial scenario of the Punjab is its small-sized industrial units. There are 194,000 small scale industrial units in the state in addition to 586 large and medium units.

Important Industries

Industrial units in the state are namely divided into three:

1. Agro-based industrial units: These may be classified as food products, beverages, cotton, wood and paper industries.
2. Machinery units
3. Chemical units

Some notable industries are:

Cotton Textile Industry

Punjab produces about 70 percent of the best quality cotton in India. The easy availability of the raw material facilitates the localisation of this industry in Punjab. In spite of several advantages, there is one main disadvantage that the total spindlage capacity of the state is only 1.5 percent of the country.

The cotton mills are located at Abohar, Malout, Phagwara, Amristar, Kharar and Ludhiana. Malerkotla, Abohar, Malout and Bhatinda are important for cotton ginning and pressing and about 25.3 lakh bales of cotton are pressed annually over here. About 97 million kgs of yarn and 36.5 million metres of cloth were produced in the cotton textile mills of Punjab.

Sugar Industry

The Sugar mills in Punjab are located at Batala, Gurdaspur, Bhogpur, Phagwara, Nawanshahar, Zira, Morinda, Rakhra, Dhuri, Fazilka, Nakodar, Budhewal, Bhatinda and Jagraon.

A salient feature of the Sugar industry is that out of the 14 mills,12 are in the Co-operative sector and only two are privately owned. Compared to Uttar Pradesh and some other states, the size of the sugar mills in Punjab is small. The Co-operative sugar mill at Morinda is the biggest in the state with a daily crushing capacity of 4,000 tonnes of sugarcane.

Dairy Industry

The primary source of milk and other dairy products in the state is the buffalo. Punjab ranks at the top in the country is the availability of milk. A major part of the milk produced in the state is consumed at the individual household level, only a limited quantity of milk is produced and processed in the milk plant.

In Punjab there are milk plants in the Public Sector, Private sector and Co-operative sector. The plants are mainly located at Verka (Amristar district), Ludhiana, Mohali, Jalandhar, Patiala, Hoshiarpur, Gurdaspur, Ferozepur, Sangrur, Bhatinda, Faridkot, Nabha, Moga, Kot Kapura and Hamira.

The plant at Moga, known as Food Specialities, is the biggest plant in the state with a processing capacity of 435 thousand litres of milk. This plant produces a variety of milk products like ghee, sweets, lassi, etc.

Vanaspati Ghee Industry

The Vanaspati ghee industry is based mainly on the production of groundnut. This industry is not very big, as the oilseeds for the country are brought from other states. The Vanaspati ghee units are situated at Amritsar, Ludhiana, Khanna, Doraha and Rajpura.

Woolen Textile Industry

Woolen textile industries are situated at Amritsar, Ludhina and Dhariwal.

Hosiery Industry

Punjab leads the whole of the country in the manufacture of hosiery products. Most of these units are located in Ludhiana. This industry is a major foreign exchange earner.

Sports Goods Industry

The sports goods industry of Punjab became well known only after 1947. Jalandhar is the main centre for the production of sports goods. This industry play a major part in earning foreign exchange.

Engineering Industries

In the absence of basic minerals, the heavy engineering industry is almost absent in the state.

a. *Bicycles:* Punjab now ranks at the top of the bicycle industry. Main centres are Ludhiana and Rajpura.

b. *Sewing Machines:* Punjab not only fulfils the home requirements for sewing machines but also exports the same. Ludhiana and Bassi Pathana are important centres for the production of sewing machines and machine parts.

c. *Agricultural Implements and Machine Tool:* The important centres for manufacture of agricultural implements are Batala, Ludhiana, Phillaur, Jalandhar, Phagwara, Goraya and Amristar.

d. *Tractors and Combines:* The state has a tractor plant at Mohali and a combine harvester plant at Bhadson.

Feed Industry and Concentrates

To develop livestock and poultry industries, it is of utmost importance to develop the feed industry on a priority basis. The possible sources of feed and concentrates are oilseed cakes and the by-products of milling and the cereals.

Wheat Bran

This is a by-product of the roller flour mills and there are about 11 such mills in the state.

Oilseed Cakes

The cotton seed is preferred as such by the farmers for feeding the milk animals. Cotton seed is utilised for oil production which is a costly product and is in great demand.

Rice Milling

About 80 percent of the paddy produced in Punjab is marketed and processed in different types of rice mills. There are about 2,200 hullers mostly in rural area, 148 shellers and 43 hullers-cum-shellers. The major by-products of rice milling are two percent germ, five percent bran and 23 percent husk

Wheat Milling

There are about 15 roller flour mills in the Punjab with a capacity of flour lakh tonnes. Local consumption of wheat is to the tune of 20 lakh tonnes, mostly as atta.

Bakery

The bakery industry is in its infant stage. There are mechanised bakery units in the Punjab which produce biscuits and bread.

Barley Processing and Malting

Barley is the chief cereal which is prepared for malting.

There are two malt factories in Punjab. Considerable export of malt extract is now contracted by a Punjab malt factory.

Maize Processing

Two private factories in Punjab manufacture starch and starch products from maize. One modern maize processing plant has been set up at Sangrur. Cornflakes is a popular breakfast food which can be manufactured as part of the maize processing mills in the malt factories. It is also possible to utilize maize for malting purposes.

Cereal based Nutritive Foods

Manufacture of nutritive food is important to counter the widely prevalent malnutrition. Several high protein rich foods such as Bal-Ahar, Multi-purpose food, Nutro Biscuits, Bulgar wheat, Vegetable Milk and Fortified Bread can be produced.

Cotton Seed Crushing

Cotton seed is highly valued for its protein and oil contents. It is high in protein and its oil content varies from 12 to 18 percent. Besides extracting oil, protein-rich flour can also be produced.

Meat and Poultry Processing

One modern chicken dressing plant was installed at Chandigarh. Other such plants are in Ludhiana, Jalandhar and Amristar.

Fruit and Vegetable Processing

Punjab has a good market for pickles and preservers. It has wide scope for processing units for the production of juice concentrates and dehydration factories for vegetables.

ECONOMY OF PUNJAB

According to the *2008 Global Hunger Index,* Punjab has the lowest level of hunger in India. Less than one-fourth of children below the age of five are underweight, although Punjab "came off worse than countries like Gabon and Vietnam when measured on the index".

Punjab has relatively good infrastructure. This includes road, rail, air and river transport links that are extensive throughout the region. Punjab has also one of the lowest poverty rate in India at 6.16% (1999-2000 figures), and has won the best state performance award, based on statistical data compiled by the Indian Government. In 2012, the state was one of the highest receiver of overall remittances to India which stood at $66.13 billion (4547429450000.00 Indian Rupees), below Kerala and Tamil Nadu.

Macro-economic trend

This is a chart of trend of gross state domestic product of Punjab at market prices estimated by *Ministry of Statistics and Programme Implementation* with figures in millions of Indian Rupees. The traditional long-term financial policy of the Union Government is to reward well-performing States.

Year	Gross State Domestic Product (Indian Rupee / Ten Million / Crores)
1980	50,250
1985	95,060
1990	188,830
1995	386,150
2000	660,100
2005	925,380
2011	2,213,320

The state's debt was estimated at 62 per cent of its GDP in 2005.

Major industrial cities

Dera Bassi, Jalandhar, Amritsar, Ludhiana, Patiala, Bathinda, Batala, Khanna, Faridkot, Rajpura, Mohali, Mandi Gobindgarh, Ropar, Firozpur, Sangrur, Malerkotla and Moga are major financial and industrialized cities. A big share of state's GDP comes from these cities.

Agriculture

Punjab (the five rivers region) is one of the most fertile regions on earth. The region is ideal for growing wheat crop. Rice, sugar cane, fruits and vegetables are also grown. Indian Punjab is called the "Granary of India" or "India's bread-basket." Many records mistakenly mention that it produces 43% of India's wheat, but that is actually its contribution to the national pool. It produces 17% of India's wheat, and 11% of India's rice (2013 data). The total area of Punjab is just 1.4% of total area of India, but it produces roughly 12% of the cereals produced in the country. The largest grown crop is wheat. Other important crops are rice, cotton, sugarcane, pearl millet, maize, barley and fruits. The principal crops of Punjab are barley, wheat, rice, maize and sugarcane. Among the fodder crops are bajra and jowar. In the category of fruits, it produces abundant stock of kinnow. The main sources of irrigation are canals and tube wells. The *rabi* or the spring harvest consists of wheat, gram, barley, potatoes and winter vegetables. The *Kharif* or the autumn harvest consists of rice, maize, sugarcane, cotton and pulses. Agriculture sector is the largest contributor to the gross state domestic product (GSDP) of Punjab. According to 2013-14 data, the contribution of agriculture and allied industries in GSDP at factor cost is 28.13%.

Industry

The state has essentially an agrarian economy with a lower industrial output as compared to other states of India. A prominent feature of the industrial scenario of the Punjab is its small sized industrial units. There are nearly 194,000 small scale industrial units in the state in addition to 586 large and medium units.Dera Bassi, Ludhiana is an important center for industry. In the 1980s there was a chance of a Hero Honda and Maruti Suzuki plant to be set up in Ludhiana but due to some circumstances of terrorism it was cancelled.

Important industries

The industrial units in the state are broadly divided into three-

- Agro-based industrial units
- Machinery units
- Chemical units

Textile industry

The state produces nearly 25% of the best quality cotton in India. In spite of several advantages, there is one major disadvantage that the total spindlage capacity of the state is only 1.5% of the country.Dera Bassi, Ludhiana is known as manchester of India. Batala was once called as "Iron bird of Asia" as it produced the highest amount of C.I.Casting, Agricultural and mechanical machinery. Batala is still one of the leading cities in Northern India in manufacturing of C.I Casting and mechanical machinery. It's also an agricultural marketplace and industrial center. Cotton ginning, weaving, sugar refining, rice milling are some of other business taking place here.

The cotton mills are located at Abohar, Malout, Phagwara, Amritsar, Kharar, Mohali and Ludhiana. Malerkotla, Abohar, Malout and Bhatinda are important for cotton ginning and pressing and nearly 25.3 million (25,300,000) bales of cotton are pressed annually over here. About 97 million kilograms of yarn and 36.5 million metres of cloth were produced in the cotton textile mills of Punjab. But only 43% of the cotton yarns formed in Punjab is used within the states and the remaining is sold outside the state. Pesticides introduced in the Green Revolution played an important part in the bustling cotton industry. The most common biopesticides in Punjab are Bacillus thuringiensis (*Bt*). With the introduction of *Bt*cotton, the total Punjab cotton area increased from 449,000 hectares in 2002 to 560,000 hectares in 2005. During this time frame, production of cotton has also increased: from 1.08 million bales (170 kg each) to 2.2 million bales, making up about 11-12% of the country's total production of cotton. Overall textile production of Punjab is predictable at Rs.105000 Million, as well as Rs.32500 Million sell abroad of knitwear, shawls, made-ups (bed sheets, pillow cases, duvet covers, and curtains) and yarns.

The direct and indirect employ of textile doings in the state of Punjab is predictable at 2 Million people. "Said Mr H.S.Cheema, Chairman, Punjab committee, Northern India Textile Mills Association (NITMA)".

Sugar industry

The sugar mills in Punjab are located at Batala, Gurdaspur, Bhogpur, Phagwara, Nawanshahr, Zira, Morinda, Rakhra, Dhuri, Fazilka, Nakodar, Dasua, Budhewal, Budhladha, Mukerian, Tarn Taran, Ajnala, Faridkot, Jagraon, Amloh, Patran and Lauhka.

Butter Sivian Near Baba Bakala One of the salient feature of the sugar industry is that out of the 22 mills, 15 are in the Co-operative sector and 7 are privately owned. Compared to the state of Uttar Pradesh and some other Indian states, the size of the sugar mills in Punjab is small. The Co-operative sugar mill at Morinda is the biggest in the state with a daily crushing capacity of 4,000 tonnes of sugarcane. Six of the cooperative sugar mills are inoperative while the remaining nine crush cane during the season which is about 150 days.

Dairy industry

The primary source of milk and other dairy products in the state is the buffalo. The state ranks at the top in the country in the availability of milk after Haryana and gujarat.

The milk plants are mainly located at Verka (Amristar district), Ludhiana, Mohali, Jalandhar, Patiala, Hoshiarpur, Gurdaspur, Ferozepur, Sangrur, Bhatinda, Faridkot, Nabha, Moga, Kot Kapura and Hamira. The plant at Moga is the biggest plant in the state with a processing capacity of nearly 435 thousand litres of milk. The first AMUL milk plant of Punjab state was opened in 2015 at Batala.

Power

Total energy of the state is provided by the PSPCL own THermal Plants a) 1260MW GURU GOBIND SINGH SUPER THERMAL PLANT at Ropar, b) 440MW Guru Nanak Dev Thermal Plant at Bhatinda, c) 920MW Guru Hargobind Thermal Plant at Lehra Mohabbat and its own Hydro Power Plants i) 110MW Shanan Power house at Joginder Nagar,ii) 600MW Ranjit Sagar DAM at Shah Pur Kandi,iii) 91.35MW UBDC power houses, iV) 207MW Mukerian Hydel Project, v) 134MW Anand Pur Sahib Hydel Channel, vi) Mini and Micro Hydro Power Plants on Sirhind Canal and its ditributeries.IN addidion to that it gets its share from Yhdro Power Plants under the control of BBMB. a) 1325MW Bhakra Dam Left and Right Bank Power Houses b) 155MW Hydro Power Plants on Bhakra Main Line at Ganguwal and Kotla, c) 396MW Hydro Power Plant at Pong, d)990MW Power Plant at Dehar.

A new Thermal plant is set up in Rajpura(Punjab) with 1400 megawatt of power capacity inaugurated on 8 December 2013. Another Thermal Plant in Bathinda with capacity of 1980 Megawatt power will come up soon.

The common pool projects are the Bhakra Nangal Complex, the Dehar Power Plant and the Pong Power Plant. Punjab shares about 51% of the Power generated from the Bhakra Nangal Complex. 48% from the Power generated at the Pong Project.

TRANSPORT

Public transport in Punjab is provided by buses, auto rickshaws, Indian railways and an international rail connection to Pakistan (Samjhauta Express). The state has a large network of multi modal transportation systems.

Punjab has six civil airports including two international airports: Amritsar International Airport and Chandigarh International Airport; and four domestic airports: Bathinda Airport, Pathankot Airport, Patiala Airport, Sahnewal Airport.

A DMU Train in Ludhiana

The Indian Railways' Northern Railway line runs through the state connecting most of the major towns and cities. The railway network in the state is controlled by Northern Railway zone divisional headquarter: Firozpur railway division and Ambala railway division.

The Shatabdi Express, India's fastest series of train connects Amritsar to New Delhi covering total distance of 449 km. Bathinda Junction is the largest railway station in the state. Punjab's major railway stations are Ludhiana Junction (LDH), Jalandhar Cantonment (JRC), Firozpur Cantonment(FZR), Jalandhar City Junction (JUC), Pathankot Junction (PTK), Amritsar Junction (ASR), Patiala railway station (PTA), SAS Nagar Mohali(SASN), Moga railway station (MOGA), Gurdaspur railway station (GSP), and Phagwara railway station (PGW).

The railway stations of Amritsar is included in the Indian Railways list of 50 world-class railway stations. The Samjhauta Express is a joint venture between Indian Railways and Pakistan Railways and runs from Attari railway station near Amritsar in India to Lahore Railway Station in Punjab, Pakistan. All the cities and towns of Punjab are connected by four-lane national highways. The Grand Trunk Road, also known as "NH1", connects Kolkata to Peshawar, passing through Jalandhar and Amritsar. Another major national highway connects Punjab to Jammu, passing through Hoshiarpur and Pathankot. National highways passing through the state are ranked the best in the country with widespread road networks that serve isolated towns as well as the border region. Ludhiana and Amritsar are among several Indian cities that have the highest accident rates in India.

There are also a bus rapid transit system Amritsar BRTS in the holy city of Amritsar, popularly known as 'Amritsar MetroBus' The following national highways connect major towns, cities and villages:

- National Highway 1
- National Highway 10
- National Highway 15
- National Highway 1A
- National Highway 20
- National Highway 21
- National Highway 22
- National Highway 64
- National Highway 70
- National Highway 71
- National Highway 95

7

Tourism

INTRODUCTION

Tourism is a swiftly expanding area and many analysts predict huge potential. Tourism of Punjab is principally suited for the tourist interested in culture, civilization, spirituality and epic history. More specifically tourism is particularly suited for the person who is interested in epic history, the celebrated Punjabi culture, royal Punjabi palaces, historic battles and of course the world-renowned examples of Sikh Architecture, shrines and temples.

The tourism sector in Punjab, India is quite developed and the state government has taken several steps to encourage the growth of the tourism and hospitality industry in Punjab-the land of five rivers.

There are several places in Punjab, India that form an important part of the tourist circuit and these are Amritsar, Jalandhar, Chandigarh, Ropar, Bhatinda, Pathankot, Muktsar, Hoshiarpur, Fatehgarh Sahib, Patiala and Kapurthala.

The tourism sector in the state of Punjab, India tries to popularize the culture and traditions of Punjab such as the local art forms like ballads of love, folk dances like the bhangra and the gidda. The colourful and vibrant Punjabi culture is reflected in the local festivals such as Baisakhi, Dussehra and Diwali.

When one speaks of Punjab, India one conjures up an elegant and beautiful picture of acres and acres of fields and prosperous farmers moving about in their tractors going about their daily chores. The state tourism sector also makes efforts to promote the traditional and local handicrafts of Punjab, India. Punjab, India is known for its wonderfully carved furniture, hand-woven scarves, rugs and durries. The local Punjabi carpenters are famous for the lovely furniture especially low seats known as peeras and peerian and artistically carved bedposts.

Punjab in India is the perfect traveller's dream. This North Indian state is the king of spicy and delicious gourmet and is nothing but a shopper's paradise. Among the cities of Punjab, India you must make it a point to visit Chandigarh during your tours. Chandigarh is a completely planned city, designed by the French architect Le Cobusier.

While on tour to Chandigarh in Punjab, India you must visit the Maha Chandi Devi Temple that is an important tourist destination in this town. The lovely landscaped gardens and the modern buildings are definitely a sight to behold for the discerning traveller.

The state tourism sector is taking steps to promote tourism in place like Amritsar and Hoshiarpur in Punjab, India. Fatehgarh Sahib in Ludhiana in Punjab, India is known for its serene beauty and the ancient Gurudwara that happens to be an important tourist destination.

The Punjab state is one of the most productive regions of India with its extensive cultivation and it also has a number of thriving Industries. It is famous for the Golden temple in Amristar which is a sacred place for the Sikhs.

Tourism in Indian Punjab centres around the historic palaces, battle sites, and the great Sikh architecture of the state and the surrounding region. Examples include various sites of the Indus Valley Civilization, the ancient fort of Bathinda, the architectural monuments of Kapurthala, Patiala, and Chandigarh, the modern capital designed by Le Corbusier.

Moti Bagh Palace in Patiala

Harmandir Sahib in Amritsar is a major tourist destination in Punjab

The Golden Temple in Amritsaris one of the major tourist destinations of Punjab and indeed India, attracting more visitors than the Taj Mahal, Lonely Planet Bluelist 2008 has voted the Harmandir Sahib as one of the world's best spiritual sites. Moreover, there is a rapidly expanding array of international hotels in the holy city that can be booked for overnight stays. Devi Talab Mandir is a Hindu temple located in Jalandhar. This temple is devoted to Goddess Durga and is believed to be at least 200 years old. Another main tourist destination is religious and historic city of Sri Anandpur Sahib where large number of tourists come to see the Virasat-e-Khalsa (Khalsa Heritage Memorial Complex) and also take part in Hola Mohalla festival. Kila Raipur Sports Festival is also popular tourist attraction in Kila Raipur near Ludhiana. Shahpur kandi fort, Ranjit sagar lake and Sikh Temple in Sri Muktsar Sahib are also popular attractions in Punjab. Punjab also has the world's first museum based on the Indian Partition of 1947, in Amritsar, called the Partition Museum.

AMRITSAR

Amritsar (Pool of Nectar) founded by the Sikh Guru Ram Dad, is named after the sacred pool of Golden temple. It is the second largest town of Punjab. It has grown from a sacred village pond into a spiritual temporal centre of Sikh culture. Amritsar is the soul of Punjab and today it is India's important distribution centre of dry-fruits. It is also the city where Jallianwala Bagh, the garden where scores of innocent Indian people were massacred by the British. Amritsar is an institution by itself. Amritsar is only 24 Kms away from Pakistani border. Travellers by land have to pass through Amritsar as it is the only way to Pakistan. The holy city of Amritsar has an extreme climate with very hot summers and very cold winters. Monsoon hits the city around the first week of July and brings average rainfall. The best time to visit Amritsar is between October and March.

The Golden Temple: The Golden Temple or 'Hari Mandir', situated in Amritsar, Punjab, is the most sacred temple of the

Sikhs. The site of the temple was sacred to the Sikhs since the time of the 4th guru, Ram Das. It is a symbol of the magnificence and strength of the Sikh people all over the world. All Sikh people tries to make a visit to the temple and take bath in holy tank of the temple.

Jallian Wala Bagh: This place noted for its most notorious massacre under British rule. It is 400 meters north of the Golden Temple. The British General Dyer was the Lieutenant Governor of the province in 1919. He banned all meetings and demonstrations led by Indians against the economical set back by World War I. On 13 April 1919, pilgrims poured into Amritsar to celebrate the Baisakhi festival, a holiday in the Sikh calendar.

In the afternoon thousands of people gathered at Jallian Wala Bagh to celebrate the Baisakhi. This ground surrounded by high walls on all sides has only a narrow alley for access. General Dyer personally led the troops to the sight and ordered his men to open fire without any warning.

It resulted in the death of 379 and injured more than 1200. India was outraged by Dyer's massacre. Gandhiji, called for a nation wide strike and started the Non-cooperation Movement, which became an important mile stone in the struggle for India's Independence. Today this ground has been changed to a park and it has a pleasant garden. There is a narrow path between the houses which leads to the lawn of the park. At the entrance there is a memorial plaque which recounts the history.

There is a well on the north side in which many people who tried to escape from the bullets were drowned, and remnants of walls have been preserved to show the bullet holes. At the east end of the garden there is a large memorial built in memory of those who died here.

Durgiana Temple: The temple is dedicated to goddess Durga and dates back to 16th century. This Hindu temple also draws its share of visitors. A large temple is dedicated to Hindu deities Laxmi (The Goddess of wealth) and Narayan. (The Preserver of Universe). All dignitaries visiting Golden Temple make it a point to visit Durgiana Temple also.

Mata Mandir: This Hindu temple situated at Rani ka Bagh, is similar to the Mata Vaishno Devi temple at Katra (Jammu). The temple draws a large number of devotees from far and near.

Fort Gobind Garh: In the south-west of the city, has been taken over by the Indian army and is now off limits. It was built in 1805-09 by Ranjit Singh, who was also responsible for constructing the city walls.

Ram Bagh: This beautiful garden is named as a tribute to Guru Ram Das, the founder of the city of Amritsar. It is situated in the new part of town and has a museum in the summer palace built by the Sikh Maharaja Ranjit Singh (1780-1839) the Lion of Punjab. The museum contains weapons dating back to Mughal times and some portraits of the ruling houses of the Punjab and a replica of the diamond 'Kohinoor'. To commemorate the memory of his valour Ram Bagh has a lively statue of Maharaja Ranjit Singh saddled on a horse. It's closed on Wednesdays.

Ram Thirth: The place gets special mention in the great Hindu epic 'Ramayana'. It is the place where Maharshi Valmiki gave shelter to Sita, wife of Rama when she was abandoned after the Lanka Victory. It was here that she gave birth to the twins Lav- Kush. There is a temple here.

Taren Taran: It is an important Sikh tank about 25km south of Amritsar. There's a temple, which predates Amritsar, and a tower on the east side of the tank, which was also constructed by Ranjit Singh. It's said that any leper who can swim across the tank will be miraculously cured.

JALANDHAR

Jalandhar, formerly Jullundhar is an ancient city in Punjab located 80 km away from Amritsar. Ruled by the Hindus and the Mughals in succession it is believed to be the oldest city in Punjab. Jalandhar today is a highly industrialized centre being India's foremost producer of world class sports equipments. The city also has the distinction of producing some of the best sportsmen in the country. Its satellite towns; Phagwara is famous for cloth manufacturing and drapery shops and Kartarpur is one of the biggest exporters of quality furniture.

PLACES OF INTEREST

Imam Nasir Mausoleum and Jamma Masjid: The 800 year old beautifully designed mausoleum of Imam Nasir is located in the heart of Jalandhar. The Jama Masjid nearby is said to be 400 years old.

Devi Talab Mandir: Devi Talab Mandir is located about one km from the railway station. The old Devi Talab has been renovated and in its centre, a new temple has been built. Recently a model of Amarnath Yatra has been built in the premises. An old temple of goddess Kali also stands by the side of the Devi Talab. The gilded Mandir is famous for the 'Hariballabh Sangeet Sammelan' held every year in December at its precincts for the past 125 years. Famous classical music exponents-both instrumental and vocal come together and perform at this gathering. In Devi Talab, there is a large masonry 200 year old tank sacred to Hindus.

Shiv Mandhir: The temple situated at Gur Mandi near Imam Nasir mausoleum dates back to the Lodhi Era. Believed to be built by the Nawab of Sultanpur Lodhi, the mandir is a blend of Muslim Hindu architecture. The main gate is built in the style of a mosque while the rest of the building is in Hindu style. There is a legend that when Jalandhar was Nawabs territory, he had eyed a newly married Hindu girl who was a devotee of Lord Shiva. Lord Shiva in the form of a serpent saved her honour. Awed by the appearance of this serpent the Nawab apologised to the girl and built the temple on her bidding.

Sodal Mandir: Thousands of devotees throng this temple during 'Anand Chaturdashi' in September. The child Deity here is believed to grant wishes of devotees.

Gurdwara Chhevin Padshahi: The sixth Guru of the Sikhs, Guru Hargobind visited Jalandhar during his tour of Doaba area and he was interviewed by a holy Muslim saint,

Shaikh Darvesh. Gurdwara Chhevin Padshahi in Basti Shaikh, is situated at the same spot where the talk was held. The great Guru had in depth discussion with Shaikh Darvesh about spiritual matters which created good impact on the holy man. A handwritten copy of Sri Guru Granth Sahib prepared sometime between 1715 and 1728 by the great Sikh scholar and martyr Baba Deep Singh is kept here.

St Mary's Cathedral Church: St Mary's Cathedral with its rare cosmo-culture design is a tribute to the Punjabi tradition. This Cathedral at Jalandhar Cantonment, initiated by representatives of His Holiness Pope John Paul II is the only one of its kind in the East. The old church dedicated to St. Patrick was built in 1947 and the foundation stone for the new church was laid in 1986.

Tulsi Mandir: Tulsi Mandir, earlier known as Temple of Vrinda, is an ancient monument in the city located in the Kot Kishan Chand locality. It was built in honour of Vrinda, wife of the demon Jalandhara. The tank on the side of the temple is said to have been the bathing place of Jalandhara.

Desh-Bhagat Memorial Hall: Desh-Bhagat Memorial Hall has been constructed to perpetuate the memory of martyrs who has lost their lives in the fight for freedom from the British rule.

Wonder Land: Wonderland Theme Park is an amusement water park with water games and water rides. The Park spreads over 11 acres with many thrilling rides offering healthy entertainment to all age groups. The park is located about 6 kms from Jalandhar Bus terminus and 8 kms from the Railway Station on Nakodar Road. The water rides includes bumper cars, flying jets, horror house, boating, kiddies' boating, play house, flying dragon and a slide splash.

The wave pool is another attraction of the water park. There is an aqua dance floor, where boys and girls enjoy dancing on the tunes of the latest Punjabi hit numbers underneath a canopy that has artificial clouds from where the water comes down like a rainfall. Entrance time is between 9.00am to 10.00pm in dry park and 12.00pm to 8.00pm in water park. Dry Park is open throughout the year. Waterpark is closed in winters as it is not inconvenient to play around in water.

CHANDIGARH

Chandigarh, the 1st planned modern city of India designed by the French architect Le Corbusier serves as the capital of both Punjab and Haryana. However, the city does not belong to either state. Chandigarh was constituted as a union territory on 1st November, 1966 and is administered by the Government of India. The city is named after the mother goddess of power, Chandi, and a fort or 'garh' beyond the Chandi temple. The city is divided into 47 numbered sectors. It has well-laid roads lined with rows of trees and beautifully planned buildings. Against the backdrop of the Siwalik smountains, the city looks charming. Chandigarh experiences extreme climate. Best time to visit this place is October to March.

Rock Garden: The Rock Garden sprawling over 64 acres is a strange but unique garden- an artists dream, build by one man's effort, love, ingenuity and skill. Nek Chand who was an ordinary public works department employee of the Chandigarh administration, conceived the idea of the garden as a solution to the disposal of city waste and domestic garbage. There are no flowers or plants in this garden. The garden was created sector by sector with rocks and discarded objects like bottle tops, fluorescent lights, mud guard, tin cans, broken glass, etc. which Nek Chand meticulously collected from door to door. The creative artist built, dolls and figures of birds, men and women and set them along a maze of paths. He was duly honoured and appointed as the director of the garden. The garden is open from 10.00 a.m to 7.00 p.m all days except Thursdays and official holidays.

Sukhna Lake: Sukna lake an artificial, man-made lake spread over 3 square kilometers on the northern border of Chandigarh is the venue of the Asian rowing championships. The tree-shaded shores is a favourite spot for strolling and bird watching. From December through February, one can see many species of aquatic birds from Central Asia and Siberia. Sukhna lake has facility for renting rowing boats and there is also a children's park.

The Open Hand Monument: Open Hand monument in the Capital Complex in sector 1, is made of a metal sheet, 14 metres high and weighing 50 tonnes and rotate freely in the wind from a high concrete pedestal.

Some times it resembles a bird in flight The design of this giant hand emblem was conceived by Le Corbusier. The symbol stands for peace and unity-'Open to give-Open to receive'. It is official emblem of the city.

Secretariat: It is the largest building in the Government or Capital Complex. It is an elongated building, with concrete walls intended as a work place for about 4000 people. The centre portion contains the offices of ministers. From the roof top of this building there is a good panoramic view of the city and the hills beyond. It cost around 14 million rupees to build. There conducted tours every 30 minutes.

The Legislative Assembly: The Legislative Assembly square in plan with a monumental portico standing free from the main building has a removable dome and a mural by Le Corbusier. It faces the high court which delineates the south eastern end of the Capitol Piazza.

The High Court: The High Court is a classic work of modern architecture. It is one of the first monuments to be built in the Capital complex. The structure of this building has a double roof, projecting over the office block, like a inverted umbrella shading its lower part, symbolizing the law as an umbrella of shelter for the ordinary citizen.

Gardens and Valleys: The Chandigarh horticulture department has done its best in turning whatever land available into beautiful landscapes. They have collected and planted varieties of ornamental plants of various colours and shades. A few places that have been turned into beautiful gardens and valleys are:

Leisure Valley: This Valley contains the famous Dr. Zakir Rose garden, Shanty Kunj, Cannas garden; the garden of unusual plants.

Dr. Zakir Rose Garden: The rose garden in sector 16 is claimed to be the Asia's largest Rose garden. This garden was created in 1967, under the expert guidance of Dr. M. S. Randhawa, Chandigarh's first Chief Commissioner, and is named after India's President, Zakir Hussain.

It is spread over an area of 30 acres and have 1600 different species of roses. Every year a 'Rose Festival' is celebrated at this garden, either at the end of February or beginning of March. It is one of the main cultural events of the city and draws thousands of visitors. There are lots of competitions, cultural celebrations and many other events.

Shanti Kunj: Shanti Kunj (Abode of Peace) situated in sector 16 has trees, streams and meditation nooks, spread over 18 acres of land.

Bougainvillea Garden: Hundreds of bougainvillea varieties adorn the garden spread over 20 acres in sector 10. The creepers cover a wide assortment of arches, pavilions and arcades. The annual Bougainvillea Show is held here.

Terraced Garden: Terraced Garden, spread over 8 acres in sector 33, is the venue for the annual Chrysanthemum Show. There is also an illuminated musical fountain here.

Topiry Garden : A garden of animals of wire figure, which is a source of amusement for the children.

Mango Gardens: (1) On Purva Marg where best quality Dusehari plants brought from Malihabad have been planted (2) Mango garden near railway station

Rajendra Park: A natural park where Mangoes, peaches, plums, etc. have been planted. Horse shows are held here from time to time.

MUSEUMS AND GALLERIES

Museum and Art Gallery: The art gallery in Sector 10, contains a modest collection of Indian stone sculptures dating back to the Gandhara period, together with some miniatures paintings and modern art. The adjacent museum has fossils and implements of prehistoric humans found in India. Visiting Hours:10.00 a.m. to 04.30. p.m. all days except Monday and official holidays.

Museum of Evolution of Life (Science Museum): Inaugurated on 14 August, 1973, this museum depicts the origin of the earth and the evolution of life. The exhibits cover 5,000 years of Indian History from the Indus Valley Civilization to the present day. There are other galleries of astronomy, geology and the world of ancient man. Visiting Hours:10.00 a.m. to 04.30. p.m. all days except Monday and official holidays.

Child Art Gallery: This gallery exhibits works by young artists of Chandigarh. The museum frequently organises art workshops for students and children. Visiting Hours:10.00 a.m. to 04.30. p.m. all days except Monday and official holidays.

National Gallery of Portraits: Situated on Sector 17B this gallery contains portraits of Indian freedom fighters, rare documents, sculptures, ceramic murals and recordings of the voices of 125 prominent figures of India's Independence movement. The library here has books on India's freedom struggle. Visiting Hours: 09.00 a.m. to 05.00 p.m. all days except Saturday & Sunday and official holidays.

International Dolls Museum: This museum situated in Bal Bhawan in Sector 23, contains more than 300 dolls from nearly every country in the world. It was inaugurated on 24th December, 1985. Visiting Hours: 09.00 a.m. to 05.00 p.m. all days except official holidays.

8

Population and Religion

POPULATION OF PUNJAB

Punjab is located in Northern India, surrounding some portion of the greater Punjab region. The state is bordered by Jammu and Kashmir, Himachal Pradesh, Haryana, Rajasthan and the Pakistani area of Punjab. Its capital is Chandigarh, a Union Territory besides the capital of the neighbouring province of Haryana.

After 1947, the Punjab region of British India was apportioned among India and Pakistan. The Indian Punjab was partitioned in 1966 with the advancement of Haryana and Himachal Pradesh alongside the current state with Punjab. Punjab is the solitary Sikh dominated state in India. Punjab is also widely known for its ever delicious food items and one should try all the delicacies when being in Punjab.

As indicated by the 2011 Indian Census, the number of inhabitants in Indian Punjab is 27,704,236.

Talking about population, in order to check out the population of Punjab in 2018, we need to have a look at the population of the past 5 years. They are as per the following:

1. 2013 – 28.4 Million
2. 2014 – 28.7 Million
3. 2015 – 29.1 Million
4. 2016 – 29.6 Million

5. 2017 – 29,924 Million

Predicting the 2018 population of Punjab is not easy but we can get the idea after analysing the population from the year 2013 – 17. As we have seen that every year the population increases by 0.2448 approximate Million people. Hence, the population of Punjab in 2018 is forecast to be 29,924 Million + 0.2448 Million = 30, 1688 Million. So, the population of Punjab in the year 2018 as per estimated data is 30, 1688 Million. Punjab Population 2018 –30, 1688 Million. (estimated).

Demography Of Punjab

The literacy rate of the state is 75%, with male literacy is 80.23% and female literacy level is 68.36%. As of the 2011 data records, the sex proportion of the state was 895 females for 1000 males. It has the second least sex proportion among other states of the nation. Since the state is into horticultural state, a broad piece of the population lives in rustic regions. Roughly 66% of the people live in country zones while the other 34% are urban tenants.

Sikhism is the main religion in Punjab, followed by 58% of the population. Hinduism is placed second with 38.5%. Before the appearance of Islam and later birth of Sikhism, Hinduism was the essential religion followed by the Punjabi individuals

Population Density And Growth Of Punjab

The population density of the state is 551 persons per square kilometre. The population is growing at a better than average rate every year from the time of Independence. The number of people in Punjab in 1991 was assessed to be 20.19 million. It achieved 24.3 million preceding the end of 2001. Around 20% of total Population in Punjab is transitory from various locales in India.

Facts About Punjab:

1. It has its International Airport in Amritsar. The state is additionally very much associated with roadways, railways and aviation.

2. Agribusiness is the establishment of Punjab. The real items are wheat, rice and cotton. There are a couple of sustenance based business wanders. The state is the best producer of Wheat in India. There are a couple of other tremendous scale business enterprises.
3. The climate of Punjab is differing. It can be to a great degree cool in winters and incredibly hot in the late spring season.
4. The state is bordered by Himachal, Haryana, Rajasthan and Jammu and Kashmir. The Punjab locale in Pakistan furthermore borders Punjab.
5. Chandigarh and Amritsar, the giant focal point of Sikh pilgrimage are the two principle visitor destinations. The Golden Temple in Amritsar is the most basic essential journey of the Sikhs.

DEMOGRAPHICS

Located in Amritsar, Harmandir Sahib is the holiest shrine of Sikhism.

Lakshmi Narayan Durgiana Templein Amritsar

Languages of Punjab (2011)

Punjabi (89.82%)

Hindi (9.35%)

Others (0.83%)

Punjab is home to 2.30% of India's population; with a density of 551 persons per km. According to the provisional results of the 2011 national census, Punjab has a population of 27,704,236, making it the 16th most populated state in India. Of which male and female are 14,639,465 and 13,103,873 respectively. In the state, the rate of population growth is 13.89 percent (2011), lower than national average.

Out of total population, 37.48% people live in urban regions. The total figure of population living in urban areas is 10,399,146 of which 5,545,989 are males and while remaining 4,853,157 are females. The urban population in the last 10 years has increased by 37.48 percent. Punjabi is the sole official language of Punjab and is spoken by the majority of the population (89.82%). Hindi is spoken by 9.35% of the population.The 2011 census found OBC and Scheduled Castes to account for 22% and 31% of the population respectively. The Forward caste (includes Jat Sikhs – 21%, Brahmins, Khatris, Arains, Banias, Thakurs/Rajputs) constitutes 41% of the total population of Punjab.

There has been a constant decline in the sex ratio of the state. The sex ratio in Punjab was 895 females per 1000 males, which was below the national average of 940. The literacy rate rose to 75.84 percent as per 2011 population census. Of that, male literacy stands at 80.44 percent while female literacy is at 70.73 percent. In actual numbers, total literates in Punjab stands at 18,707,137 of which males were 10,436,056 and females were 8,271,081.

Punjab has the largest population of Sikhs in India and is the only state where Sikhs form a majority with approximately 57.69 percent of the state population practicing Sikhism as of 2011. Hinduism is second most popular religion in state of Punjab with 38.49% following it. Islam is followed by 1.93%, Christianity by 1.26%, Jainism by 0.16%, Buddhism by 0.12%. Around 0.04% stated 'Other Religion', approximately 0.32% stated No Particular Religion. Sikhs form a majority in 17 districts out of the 22. Hindus constitute the majority in 5 districts: complete majority in Jalandhar, Hoshiarpur, Nawanshahr, Pathankot districts and a marginal majority in the Gurdaspur District. Malerkotla is the only city in Punjab with a Muslim majority.

Religion in Punjab (2011)

Sikhism (57.69%)

Hinduism (38.49%)

Islam (1.93%)

Christianity (1.26%)

Jainism (0.16%)

Buddhism (0.12%)

Other or not religious (0.36%)

The Sikh shrine, Harmandir Sahib (Golden Temple), is in the city of Amritsar, which houses the SGPC, the top most Sikh religious body. The Sri Akal Takht Sahib, which is within the Golden Temple complex, is the highest temporal seat of Sikhs. Of the five Takhts (Temporal Seats of religious authority) of Sikhism, three are in Punjab. These are Sri Akal Takht Sahib,

Damdama Sahib and Anandpur Sahib. At least one Sikh Gurdwara can be found in almost every village in the state, as well as in the towns and cities (in various architectural styles and sizes). Before the advent of Islam, and later birth of Sikhism, Hinduism was the main religion practised by the Punjabi people. Due to non-exclusive nature of their religion, a segment of Punjabis who are categorised as Punjabi Hindus continue heterogeneous religious practices in spiritual kinship with Sikhism. This not only includes veneration of the Sikh Gurus in private practice but also visits to Sikh Gurdwaras in addition to Hindu temples.

DEMOGRAPHICS OF PUNJAB

According to the 2011 Census of India, Punjab has a population of around 27.7 million. Sikhism is the most practiced faith in Punjab, and 57.69% of the population belongs to the Sikh faith. Around 38.49% of the population practices Hinduism. Other faiths include Islam, Buddhism, Christianity and Jainism.

At least one Sikh Gurdwara can be found in every municipality (in various styles and sizes).

The Punjabi language, written in the Gurmukhi script is the official language of the state. Muslims form slight majority in the Malerkotla town. The Muslim population in Punjab has increased to 1.93% due to labourer workers from other Indian states, mainly Bihar and Uttar Pradesh. As of June 2018, the caste population data for each caste in Punjab collected in Socio Economic and Caste Census 2011 has not been released to public by Government of India.

RELIGIONS OF PUNJAB

Punjab is the land where a number of religions exist in perfect harmony with each other. Sikhism and Hinduism form the major religions of the state. The other religions, like Islam, Christianity, Jainism and Buddhism, also flourish, though comparatively low in proportion. Lets us check out more information on the major religions that are followed in the state of Punjab.

Sikhism

Sikhism forms the main religion of Punjab in India. Founded by Guru Nanak Dev and other nine Gurus, it forms the fifth largest religion in the world. The main faith of Sikhism is in "Waheguru", meaning the Universal God. The religion preaches attainment of salvation through disciplined and personal meditation of the Almighty. Sikhs worship the ten Gurus and Guru Granth Sahib, the Holy Scripture that is revered as the eleventh and final Guru. Sikhism stresses on monotheism and non-anthropomorphic concept of God. Charity work and community services are considered to be crucial in a person's life. Hard work and true dedication is regarded as the basic guideline to lead one's life. Punjab abounds in gurdwaras, which form the principal center of worship for the Sikhs. The Golden Temple of Amritsar is a world famous pilgrimage center, which attracts flocks of devotees from across the globe.

Hinduism

Hinduism, though not as widely prevalent as the Sikhism, is a prominent religion of Punjab. In fact, it is the second most prominent religion practiced in the state. The Hindus have a liberal lifestyle and most of them even worship in gurdwaras. They are mostly into trade and commerce. The most common castes in Hinduism, as prevalent in Punjab, are Khatri (Kshatriya in Hindi), Brahman, Baniya and Rajput. The important Hindu sects are the Sanatan Dharmis, Arya Samajis, Radhaswamis, Nanak Panthis and Ecumenical Hinduism.

Others

Islam forms another important religion in Punjab, though there is only a minority following the same. After the partition in 1947, most of the Muslims in Punjab migrated to Pakistan. Despite the few followers of Islam, one can easily find good number of mosques in the state. Christianity, Jainism and Buddhism form other minority religions of the state.

RELIGION – SIKHISM

Religion has played an important role in shaping Punjabi ethnic identity and it is not uncommon for Punjabis to generally treat their religious identity as synonymous with their ethnic identity or at least a combined identity that differentiates them from others. Punjabis belong largely to three major religions, Islam, Hinduism and Sikhism. The majority of Punjabis are Muslims, Sikhism is also a major religion followed by Punjabi's in India. A large number of Punjabis in Pakistan are also Christian and a small number in India are Jains.

Sikhism is a religion that began in sixteenth century Northern India with the teachings of Nanak and nine successive human gurus. This system of religious philosophy and expression has been traditionally known as the Gurmat (literally *the teachings of the gurus*) or the Sikh Dharma. *Sikhism* comes from the word *Sikh*, which in turn comes from the Sanskrit root *[ikya* meaning "disciple" or "learner", or *[ikha* meaning "instruction." Sikhism is the ninth-largest religion in the world, and is generally considered the fifth largest organized religion, depending on how one defines an "organized religion".

The principal belief in Sikhism is faith in *Vahigurû*— represented using the sacred symbol of *–k MaEkar*. Sikhism advocates the pursuit of salvation through disciplined, personal meditation on the name and message of God. The followers of Sikhism are ordained to follow the teachings of the ten Sikh gurus, or enlightened leaders, as well as the holy scripture—the *Guru Granth Sahib*—which includes the selected works of many authors from diverse socioeconomic and religious backgrounds.

The text was decreed by Gobind Singh, the tenth guru, as the final guru of the Khalsa Panth. Sikhism's traditions and teachings are distinctly associated with the history, society and culture of the Punjab.

Adherents of Sikhism are known as Sikhs (*students* or *disciples*) and number over 23 million across the world. However, most Sikhs live in the state of Punjab in India; prior to partition, millions of Sikhs lived in what is now the Punjab province of Pakistan.

Philosophy and Teachings

Sikh religious philosophy has roots in the religious traditions of northern India.

The *Sant Mat* traditions are fundamental to the teachings of Sikhism's founder, Nanak. Especially important to the connection with Sikhism were the teachings of some of the saints such as Ravidas and Kabir.

Sikhism is also inspired by the emphasis on devotion to God in the traditions of Vaishnavism, especially through the *Bhakti* movement, as well as influences of Sufism.

However, Nanak's teachings diverge significantly from Vaishnavism in their rejection of idol worship, the doctrine of divine incarnations and a strict emphasis on inward devotion; Sikhism is professed to be a more difficult personal pursuit than *Bhakti*. The evolution of Nanak's thoughts on the basis of his own experiences and study have also given Sikhism a distinctly unique feature.

Scholars have presented Sikhism as a distinct faith. Some scholars have presented it as a syncretic religion which combines some elements of Hinduism and Islam. Sikhs maintain that their religion was directly revealed by God, and many of them consider the notion that Sikhism is a syncretic religion to be offensive.

God

In Sikhism, God – termed *Vahiguru* is formless, eternal, and unobserved: *niraEkar*, *akal*, and *alakh*. Nanak interpreted Vahiguru as a single, personal and transcendental creator.

The beginning of the first composition of Sikh scripture is the figure signifying the unity of God. To achieve salvation, the devotee must develop an intimate faith in and relationship with God.

God is omnipresent and infinite, and is signified by the term *ck oaEkar*. Sikhs believe that prior to creation, all that existed was God and his infinite *hukam* (will). When God willed, the entire cosmos was created. From these beginnings, God nurtured "enticement and attachment" to *maya*, or the human perception of reality.

While a full understanding of God is beyond human beings, Nanak described God as not wholly unknowable. God is omnipresent (*sarav viapak*) in all creation and visible everywhere to the spiritually awakened.

Nanak stressed that God must be seen from "the inward eye," or the "heart" of a human being: devotees must meditate to progress towards enlightenment.

Nanak emphasised the revelation through meditation, as its rigorous application permits the existence of communication between God and human beings. God has no gender in Sikhism, though translations may incorrectly present a masculine God. In addition, Nanak wrote that there are many worlds on which God has created life.

Pursuing Salvation

Nanak's teachings are founded not on a final destination of heaven or hell, but on a spiritual union with God which results in salvation. The chief obstacles to the attainment of salvation are social conflicts and an attachment to worldly pursuits, which commit men and women to an endless cycle of birth-a concept known as *karma.*

Maya—defined as illusion or "unreality"—is one of the core deviations from the pursuit of God and salvation-people are distracted from devotion by worldly attractions which give only illusive satisfaction.

However, Nanak emphasised maya as not a reference to the unreality of the world, but of its values. In Sikhism, the influences of ego, anger, greed, attachment and lust—known as the *Five Evils*—are to be particularly pernicious. The fate of people vulnerable to the Five Evils is separation from God, and the situation may be remedied only after intensive and relentless devotion.

Nanak described God's revelation—the path to salvation—with terms such as *nam* (the divine *Name*) and *œabad* (the divine Word) to emphasise the totality of the revelation.

Nanak designated the word *guru* (meaning *teacher*) as the voice of God and the source and guide for knowledge and salvation.

Salvation can be reached only through rigorous and disciplined devotion to God. Nanak distinctly emphasised the irrelevance of outwardly observations such as rites, pilgrimages or asceticism. He stressed that devotion must take place through the heart, with the spirit and the soul.

A key practice to be pursued is *nm simraG*—remembrance of the divine Name. The verbal repetition of the name of God or a sacred syllable is an established practice in religious traditions in India, but Nanak's interpretation emphasised inward, personal observance. Nanak's ideal is the total exposure of one's being to the divine Name and a total conforming to the divine Order. Nanak described the result of the disciplined application of *nm simraG* as a "growing towards and into God" through a gradual process of five stages. The last of these is *sac khaG.*

(*The Realm of Truth*)—the final union of the spirit with God.

Nanak stressed *kirat karô*-that a Sikh should balance work, worship, and charity, and should defend the rights of all creatures, and in particular, fellow human beings. They are encouraged to have a *ca[dî kala*, or *optimistic*, view of life. Sikh teachings also stress the concept of sharing—*vaG*

Chakkô—through the distribution of free food at Sikh gurdwaras (*laEgar*), giving charitable donations, and working for the betterment of the community and others (*scva*).

9

Art, Architecture, Fair and Festivals

ARTS

Punjab, 15th largest state in India is rich in its arts and Culture. People of Punjab entertain themselves in variety of ways which include dance and music and of course they are famous for their rhythmic movements and colourful dresses. Arts and crafts of Punjab is so rich, varied and versatile that even common man feels it-s charm.Most popular Punjabi Dances are Bhangra, Giddha, Jhumar, Luddi, Dankara Julli, Sammi, Dhamal, Jaago, Kikli and Gatka.

Fairs

Baba Sodal mela

A large Hindu fair is held in Jalandhar city. The fair of Baba Sodal is associated with a small boy named Sodal, who is respected as a child-god.The fair commemorates his death anniversary. The fair is held annually during December.

Rauza Sharif Urs

Rauza Sharif Urs is celebrated in the memory of Sufi Saint Sheikh Ahmed Farooqi Sirhindi who was a disciple of Khawaja Baqi Billah. The fair takes place on the Fategarh Sahib-Bassi Pathan road in Fatehgarh Sahib.

Jor Mela

Fatehgarh Sahib Gurdwara, Punjab

Annual three-day Shaheedi Jor Mela is held at Fatehgarh Sahib Gurdwara in memory of Sahibzada Zorawar Singh and Fateh Singh. Processions are taken out and Sikh games are displayed in the three-day Mela.

Bathinda Virasat Mela

The mela showcases traditional Punjabi culture at the Jaipal Theme Village inside the Bathinda Sports Stadium. The mela also involves heritage walks from Gurdwara Haji Rattan to Jaipalgarh theme village.

Vaisakhi

Local fairs are organised in various places in Punjab on Vaisakhi.

Mela Maghi

The Mela Maghi held at Muktsar lasts for three days.

Baba Sheikh Farid Aagman

Baba Farid, a 12th-century Sufi Saint, visited Faridkot, named after him. The fair takes place at Gurdwara Tilla Baba Farid and includes cultural and sporting events.

The mela takes place every year between 19 September and 23 September, Evolving from its spiritual origin associated with the visit of Sufi Prophet, the festival has now become all pervasive embracing cultural, literary, intellectual and sports spheres of the people of this region.

In the true Sufi tradition of its founder saint, the festival has inherited the gospel of Humanism, Communal Harmony and National Integration is the conspicuous theme of the Aagman Purb.

Basant Festival of Kites

Local fairs are held in various places on Basant. The ruler of Kapurthala princely state, Maharaja Jagatjit Singh, started the Basant Panchami fair which is now in its 97th year (2014). People attend the fair at Shalamar Bagh wearing yellow clothes and turbans. In Hoshiarpur, a fair is held at the Boeli of Baba Bhandari where thousands of men, women and children participated and pay obeisance at the samadhi of martyr Dharamvir Hakikat Rai. Basant in the Punjab is associated with Hakikat Rai who laid down his life to fight for the right of people to follow their religion of choice. At the fair held at the Boeli of Baba Bhandari, it is customary to hold kite flying competitions.

Festivals

Kila Raipur Sports Festival

In February every year, the Kila Raipur Sports Festival takes place showcasing bullock, dog, mules, camel and other animal races.

Around a million people attend the annual sporting event which has now become an important part of India's Punjab culture. Spectators travel from all over the world to the village of Kila Raipur to attend the games which attracts more than 4,000 sportsmen and women every February. Games include being run over by farm machinery, bullock chariot racing, horseback acrobatics and other weird demonstrations of strength.

Patiala Heritage festival

Started in 2003, the festival takes place in Patiala in the Qila Mubarak Complex, which lasts for ten days. The festival includes the Crafts Mela, Indian classical music (vocal and instrumental) and dance concerts.

Kapurthala Heritage Festival

The Baba Jassa Singh Ahluwalia Heritage Festival is held by the Kapurthala Heritage Trust, in collaboration with the Indian National Trust for Arts and Cultural Heritage and supported by the Government of Punjab. The festival takes place at Jagatjit Palace and centres on classical music, dance and theatre.

Amritsar Heritage Festival

The festival showcases bhangra, giddha, gatka troupes, horses and elephants. The cultural programmes include shabad kirtan, theatre, music and dance.

Harivallabh Sangeet Festival

Taking place every year on 27–30 December, the music festival honors the memory of Swami Harivallabh. The festival is recognised by the Government of India as a National festival of music. Harivallabh shall complete 139 Years on 28 December 2014. The festival is held at the Devi Talab Mandir in Jalandhar city

SIKH ARCHITECTURE

Sikh Architecture is a style of architecture that is characterized with values of progressiveness, exquisite intricacy, austere beauty and logical flowing lines. Due to its progressive style, it is constantly evolving into many newly developing branches with new contemporary styles.

Although Sikh architecture was initially developed within Sikhism its style has been used in many non-religious buildings due to its beauty. 300 years ago, Sikh architecture was distinguished for its many curves and straight lines; Shri Keshgarh Sahib and the Sri Harmandir Sahib (Golden Temple) are prime examples.

Further examples of Sikh architecture can be found in the countries of India, Pakistan, Afghanistan, Bangladesh, Saudi Arabia, Iraq and Turkey — these examples are mostly memorials of the places the Sikh Gurus visited. Modern examples can be found worldwide; in the Americas, Oceania Europe and Asia.

Apart from religious buildings, Sikh architecture includes secular forts, *bungas* (residential places), palaces, and colleges. The religious structure is called *gurdwara* (a place where the Guru dwells). The word *gurdwara* is a compound of *guru* (guide or master) and *dwara* (gateway or seat). So, it has an architectural connotation. Sikh *gurdwaras* are generally commemorative buildings connected with the ten gurus in some way, or with places and events of historical significance. Some examples are Gurdwara Dera Sahib (halting place), in Batala in Gurdaspur district. It was erected in memory of the brief stay of Guru Nanak along with his companions on the occasion of his marriage. Gurdwara Shahid Ganj (Martyr's Memorial) in Muktsar in Faridkot district commemorates the cremation spot of Sikhs who were killed in a battle between Guru Gobind Singh and the Mughals in 1705. Gurdwara Shish Mahal (hall of mirrors) in Kiratpur in Ropar district was made where Guru Har Kisan was born.

There are over 500 historical *gurdwaras*.

PUNJABI FESTIVALS

Punjabi festivals are various festive celebrations observed by Punjabis in Pakistan, India and the diaspora Punjabi community found worldwide. The Punjabis are a diverse group of people from different religious background that affects the festivals they observe. According to a 2007 estimate, the total population of Punjabi Muslims is about 90 million (~75% of all Punjabis), with 97% of Punjabis who live in Pakistan following Islam, in contrast to the remaining 30 million Punjabi Sikhs and Punjabi Hindus who predominantly live in India.

The Punjabi Muslims typically observe the Islamic festivals, do not observe Hindu or Sikh religious festivals, and in Pakistan the official holidays recognize only the Islamic festivals. The Punjabi Sikhs and Hindus typically do not observe these, and instead observe historic festivals such as Lohri, Basant and Baisakhi as seasonal festivals. The Sikh and Hindu festivals are regional official holidays in India, as are major Islamic festivals. Other seasonal Punjabi festivals in India include Teejon (Teeyan) and Maghi.

The Punjabi Muslim festivals are set according to the lunar Islamic calendar (Hijri), and the date falls earlier by 10 to 13 days from year to year. The Hindu and Sikh Punjabi seasonal festivals are set on specific dates of the luni-solar Bikrami calendar or Punjabi calendarand the date of the festival also typically varies in the Gregorian calendar but stays within the same two Gregorian months.

Some Punjabi Muslims participate in the traditional, seasonal festivals of the Punjab region: Baisakhi, Basant and to a minor scale Lohri, but this is controversial. Islamic clerics and some politicians have attempted to ban this participation because of the religious basis of the Punjabi festivals, and they being declared haram (forbidden in Islam).

Buddhist festivals

Punjabi Buddhists are a minority in Punjab, India. In the Punjab province of Pakistan, the Buddhist population is negligible.

Punjabi Buddhists celebrate festivals such as Buddha Jayanti.

Christian Festivals

Christians are a minority in Pakistan, constituting about 2.3% of its population in contrast to 97.2% Muslims. In Indian state of Punjab, Christians form about 1.1% of its total population, while the predominant majority of the population being Sikh and Hindus. Punjabi Christians celebrate Christmas to mark the birth of Jesus. In Punjab, Pakistan, people stay up late singing Punjabi Christmas carol services. People attend churches in places such as Gurdaspur, Amritsar, Jalandharand Hoshiarpur districts in Punjab, India that have a higher Christian population, to be part of Christmas celebrations.Christians also celebrate Easter by engaging in processions.

Hindu and Sikh festivals

Holi

Holi is the spring Hindu festival of colours which is celebrated by throwing colours on each other. The festival is celebrated on the first day of the Punjabi lunar month of Chet and marks the Spring season. The festival is primarily celebrated by Hindus. But Sikhs also participate in the festival which is seasonal in its significance and secular in its celebration.

In the Indian state of Punjab, Holi is preceded by Holika Dahan the night before. On the day of Holi, people engage in throwing colours on each other.

During Holi in Punjab, walls and courtyards of rural houses are enhanced with drawings and paintings similar to rangoli in South India, *mandana* in Rajasthan, and rural arts in other parts of India. This art is known as *chowk-poorana* or *chowkpurana* in Punjab and is given shape by the peasant women of the state. In courtyards, this art is drawn on cloth. The art includes drawing tree motifs, flowers, ferns, creepers, plants, peacocks, palanquins, geometric patterns along with vertical, horizontal and oblique lines. These arts add to the festive atmosphere.

Lohri

Lohri is a popular winter time Punjabi folk festival, celebrated primarily by Sikhs and Hindus from the Punjab region of Indian subcontinent. According to Chauhan (1995), all Punjabis, including Muslims and Christians celebrate Lohri in Punjab, India. Lohri is celebrated on the last day of the month of poh (January).

Many people believe the festival commemorates the passing of the winter solstice. Lohri is observed the night before Makar Sankranti, also known as Maghi, and according to the solar part of the lunisolar Bikrami calendar and typically falls about the same date every year (January 13).

Lohri is an official gazetted holiday in the state of Punjab (India), but it is not a holiday in Punjab (Pakistan). It is, however, observed by Sikhs and some Punjabi Muslims and Christians in Pakistan as well.

Maghi

Maghi is a Sikh festival and one of their largest annual gatherings near Gurudwaras. The same festival is called Makar Sankranti by Hindus, who gather near Hindu temples. The *Magha Mela*, according to Diana L. Eck – a professor at Harvard University specializing in Indology, is mentioned in the Hindu epic, the *Mahabharata*, thus placing this festival to be around 2,000 years old. Many go to sacred rivers or lakes and bathe with thanksgiving to the sun.

People visit the Gurdwara or the Mandir. The festival marks the increase in daylight. Maghi is celebrated by people eating kheer such as Rauh di kheer which is an old dish where rice is cooked in sugarcane juice. The dish is prepared in the evening before Maghi and is kept to cool. It is served cold next morning on Maghi with red-chilly mixed curd. In some parts of Punjab, India, it is also traditional to eat kichdi mixed with lentils, consume raw sugarcane and jaggery, Fairs are held at many places on Maghi. Sports festivals are also held in the region.

Basant Festival

Basant Festival is an ancient Hindu spring festival dedicated to god Kama as well as goddess Saraswati. Its link with the Hindu god of love and its traditions have led some scholars to call it "a Hindu form of Valentine's Day". The festival is also observed by Punjabi Sikhs. The traditional colour of the day is yellow and the dish of the day is saffron rice. People fly kites.

In North India, and in the Punjab province of Pakistan, Basant is celebrated as a spring festival of kites. The festival marks the commencement of the spring season. In the Punjab region (including the Punjab province of Pakistan), Basant Panchami has been a long established tradition of flying kites and holding fairs.

Punjabi Muslims have treated parts of the festival as a cultural event. In Pakistan however kite flying has been banned starting in 2007 with officials stating that it uses dangerous, life-threatening substances on the strings. The festival ban was confirmed by the Pakistan Punjab state chief minister Shehbaz Sharif in 2017. According to some analysts, "the festival was banned due to pressure from hardline religious and extremist groups like the Hafiz Saeed-led Jamaat-ud Dawah, which claimed the festival had "Hindu origins" and was "un-Islamic".

Vaisakhi

Vaisakhi is a religious festival of Sikhs and Hindus. Vaisakhi is also a harvest festival for people of the Punjab region. In the Punjab, Vaisakhi marks the ripening of the rabi harvest. Vaisakhi also marks the new year for Punjabi Sikhs and Hindus. Punjabi Muslims observe the new year according to the Islamic calendar. The harvest festival is celebrated by Punjabi Sikhs and Hindus.

According to Aziz-ud-din Ahmed, Lahore used to have Baisakhi Mela after the harvesting of the wheat crop in April. However, adds Ahmed, the city started losing its cultural vibrancy in 1970s after Zia-ul-Haq came to power, and in recent years "the Pakistan Muslim League (N) government in Punjab banned kite flying through an official edict more under the pressure of those who want a puritanical version of Islam to be practiced in the name of religion than anything else". Unlike the Indian state of Punjab that recognizes the Vaisakhi Sikh festival as an official holiday, the festival is not an official holiday in Punjab or Sindh provinces of Pakistan where Islamic holidays are officially recognized instead. However, On 8 April 2016, Punjabi Parchar at Alhamra (Lahore) organised a show called Visakhi mela, where the speakers pledged to "continue our struggle to keep the Punjabi culture alive" in Pakistan through events such as Visakhi Mela. Elsewhere Besakhi fairs or melas are held in various places including Eminabad and Dera Ghazi Khan.

Teeyan

Teeyan welcomes the monsoon season and the festival officially starts of the day of Teej and last for 13 days. The seasonal festival involves women and girls dancing Gidha and visiting family. The festival is observed in Punjab, India.

The festival is celebrated during the monsoon season from the third day of the lunar month of Sawan on the bright half, up to the full moon of sawan, by women. Married women go to their maternal house to participate in the festivities. In the past, it was traditional for women to spend the whole month of Sawan with their parents.

Teej is historically a Hindu festival, dedicated to Goddess Parvati and her union with Lord Shiva, one observed in northern, western, central and Himalayan regions of the Indian subcontinent.

Others

Other festivals observed by Punjabi Hindus and Sikhs include Diwali, Dussehra, Rama Navami, Bandi Chhor Divas and Gurpurabs. Raksha Bandhan in the Punjab is known as 'Rakhri' and is celebrated as a brothers and sisters day.

Muslim festivals

The following religious festivals are observed by Punjabi Muslims.

Eid ul-Adha

Eid ul-Adha is also known as Eid-ul-Azha. The festival is celebrated on the tenth day of the last Islamic month of Zilhij. Eid-ul-Azha occurs about two months after Eid-ul-Fitr. Eid-ul-Azha is celebrated to commemorate the occasion when the prophet Abraham was ready to sacrifice his son, Ismail, on God's command. Abraham was awarded by God by replacing Ismail with a goat. Muslims make pilgrimage (hajj) to Meccaduring this time.

Animal sacrifice is a tradition offered by Muslims on this day. Special markets are set up to deal with the increase in demand of animals. Cattle markets are set up in places such as Multan, (Punjab, Pakistan) and goat markets in Ludhiana, (Punjab, India). The children celebrate Eid ul-Adha and Eid ul-Fitr with great pump and show and receive gifts and Eidi (money) from parents and others.

Eid-ul-Fitr

Eid al-Fitr takes place on the first day of the tenth month of the Islamic lunar calendar and celebrates the end of Ramadan. Ramadan is the time of fasting that continues throughout the ninth month. On this day, after a month of fasting, Muslims express their joy and happiness by offering a congregational prayer in the mosques. Special celebration meals are served. The festival is celebrated in Punjab, Pakistan. It is also celebrated in Malerkotla (Punjab, India) which has a sizable Muslim population where Sikhs and Hindus also participate in the observance.

Eid-e-Milad-un-Nabi

Eid-e-Milad-un- Nabi is an Islamic festival which is celebrated in honour of the birth-day of Prophet Muhammad. The festival is observed in the third month of the Islamic lunar calendar called Rabi'al-Awal. Various processions take place in Lahore to celebrate the festival.According to Nestorovic (2016), hundreds of thousands of people gather at Minare-Pakistan, Lahore, between the intervening night of 11th and 12th Rabi' al-awwal of the Islamic calendar Eid Milad Dun Nabi. The festival was declared a national holiday in Pakistan in 1949.

People from various places in Punjab, Pakistan including Bahawalpur, Faisalabad, Multan and Sargodha participate in processions and engage in decorating Mosques, streets and houses with green flags and lights. According to Khalid, children, teenagers and young adults decorate their Pahari (mountain) of all sorts of toys, including cars, stereos, and numerous other commodities. Within various places of Lahore, there are numerous stalls. Before the festival became a celebratory day, people used to celebrate the day quietly. However, the first procession to mark the day was led from Delhi gate in Lahore in 1935. This tradition then became popular elsewhere. Processions are also taken out in Bathinda (Punjab, India).

Muharram

Remembrance of Muharram is a set of rituals associated with Shia, which takes place in Muharram, the first month of the Islamic calendar. Many of the events associated with the ritual take place in congregation halls known as *Hussainia*. The event marks the anniversary of the Battle of Karbala when Imam Hussein ibn Ali, the grandson of Muhammad, was killed by the forces of the second Umayyad caliph Yazid I at Karbala. Family members, accompanying Hussein ibn Ali, were killed or subjected to humiliation. The commemoration of the event during yearly mourning season, from first of Muharram to twentieth of Safar with Ashura comprising the focal date, serves to define Shia communal identity.

In Pakistani Punjab, Muharram is celebrated twice, once according to the Muslim year and again on the 10th of harh.

Processions

Traditionally, a white horse representing Ali's white Mule Duldul, is usually lead in the Muharram procession, as in Jhang, Punjab, Pakistan. Zuljanah, Tazia and Alam processions are observed in many places in Punjab, Pakistan including Sialkot, Gujranwala, Bahawalnagar, Sargodha, Bahawalpur. and Lahore.

Zuljana

Zuljanah processions are held which involves taking a replica of a horse. The Zuljanah has two wings and the processions were introduced from Iran to Lahore during the 19th century.

Tazia

Shia Muslims take out a Tazia procession on the day of Ashura. A Tazia is traditionally a bamboo and paper model of Hussain's tomb at Karbala, which is carried in procession by Shias on the tenth day of the month of Muharram. Moderns forms of Tazia can be more elaborate. Tazia processions in Punjab are historic and were observed during the Sikh and British period when the Tazia would be divided into many storeys, but not ordinarily more than three. Such processions take place in Lahore where mourners take to the streets to commemorate the sacrifices of Imam Hussain and his family in Karbala. Various stalls are set up offering milk, water and tea along the route of the processions. Some distribute juice packets, dry fruit, sweetmeats and food among mourners. Tazia processions can also be seen in Malerkotla and Delhi.

Alam

Alam processions take place in Punjab, Pakistan too. Alam is an elaborate, heavy battle standard, carried by a standard bearer, alam-dar, ahead of the procession. It represents Imam Hussain's standard and is revered as a sacred object.

Local festivals

Various local fairs and festivals are associated with particular shrines, temples and gurdwaras.

Mela Chiragan

Mela Chiraghan (Festival of Lights) is a three-day annual festival to mark the urs (death anniversary) of the Punjabi Sufi poet and saint Shah Hussain (1538-1599) who lived in Lahore in the 16th century. It takes place at the shrine of Shah Hussain in Baghbanpura, on the outskirts of Lahore, Pakistan, adjacent to the Shalimar Gardens.

Rath Yatra Nabha

Rath Yatra Nabha, Ratha Jatra or Chariot Festival is a Hindu festival associated with the god Jagannath held at Mandir Thakur Shri Saty Narayan Ji in the Nabha City, state of Punjab, India. This annual festival is celebrated in the month of August or September. The festival is connected to Jagannath's visit to Nabha city.

Hola Mohalla

A fair is held at Anandpur Sahib (Punjab, India) during the lunar month of Chet to celebrate the Sikh festival of Hola Mohalla. The fair is held on a very large scale every year on the day following Holi. Thousands of devotees come from all parts of the country to pay their homage to Guru Gobind Singh.

FAIRS AND FESTIVALS

The Gay and vivacious Punjabi's are very fond of fairs and festivals and almost every fortnight there is a fair or a festival in one part of the state or the other. People come to participate in such functions from far-off places, trudging dusty distances. Many a fair is held in memory of a saint or a pir, and people from all communities living in a village participate in it. Men, women and children of all ages, classes and creeds flock in hundreds and enjoy the numerous fascinating features of the fair: races, singing, wrestling bouts, acrobatics etc.

They play on folk instruments, such as Vanjli and Algoza. To a lover of culture, a Punjabi fair is an aesthetic treat. In the life of a Punjabi, fair and festivals are always an occasion to wear new clothes. Both old and young come out in their multi-coloured and smartest best. Some enthusiasts colour and brush up even their cattle and take them along.

Fairs

An average fair is enchantingly picturesque. A bustling market springs up, in which articles of food and products of local handicrafts-toys, glass bangles and an assortment of all kinds of articles for domestic use-are on display. A greater accent is, however, always on the toy shops where photographs and clay models of Rama and Sita, of Hanuman flying with the life giving herb, of Lord Krishna and his Gopis, and of Lord Siva with his trident and snakes are well displayed.

The whole mythology seems to be depicted in toys. Women can be seen excitedly haggling for trinkets. There is fun and frolic all round. The old as well as the young run to the swings and swing to their heart's content. The gay ones in small groups sing Bolian and perform folk dances to the strain of the Vanijli and Algoza. The sturdy ones test their strength in wrestling fields. It is a feast of colour and gaiety and fully reflects the joy of the community.

The fairs of the Punjab are linked with its culture and reflect by and large, the various phases of its life. Some of the distinct Punjabi traits are depicted in them. They may be divided into the following types: (i) Seasonal fairs (ii) Mythical fairs (iii) Fairs held in honour of saints (iv) Fairs connected with festivals.

Basant Panchami

Basant Panchami is the most famous of the seasonal fairs. It heralds the advent of spring. Fields of mustard present a unique and colourful sight all over rural Punjab which looks like a newly wedded damsel resplendent in her gorgeous golden yellow. There is a spirit of gay abandon in the air and the Punjabi is rightly infected with the spirit. His heart and soul become one with nature and he expresses his elevated spirit in song and dance. The Basant fair is held in many villages of the Punjab. People put on yellow costumes appropriate to the season. One huge mass of mustard blossom seems walking down to the fair. Kite-flying was a popular entertainment of the people on this occasion. Often on the Basant Panchami day, if there was a good breeze, one could see nothing but innumerable multi-coloured kites in the sky, swishing over in all directions.

Baisakhi

Baisakhi is a seasonal festival with a special accent. It is celebrated all over the state on the first of Baisakh. This is the time when harvest is gathered in and the farmer exults in the fulfillment of his year's hard work. He joins the merry-making with full gusto and does not mind walking for miles to be able to do so. Since this fair is also an expression of prosperity, singing and dancing constitute its most enchanting features. The Punjab's famous dances, Bhangra and Giddha are inextricably linked with this festival.

Many fairs in the Punjab are held near the tombs and shrines of Pirs. These fairs must have originated in a spirit of devotion to those saints and sages. People of all classes and creeds join in without any inhibition. The most famous such fairs are: the Chhapar fair, the Jarag fair and the Roshni fair of Jagranvan.

Chhapar Fair

This fair is held on Anand Chaudas, the 14th day of the bright half of Bhadon in honour of Gugga Pir. A big shrine known as 'Gugge di Marhi' has been built in his memory. The Pir was very popular in his time, and his disciples can be found all over the Punjab. He was a Chauhan Rajput and according to legend, he gently descended into the bosom of Mother Earth along with his steed, and never returned. He was believed to possess special power over all kinds of snakes. On the day this fair is held, villages scoop the earth seven times because they believe that in this way they invoke Gugga Pir to protect them against snakes. This shrine has a reputation for curing people of snake-bite. It is strongly believed that if a person is bitten by a snake, all that has to be done is to take him to the shrine and lay him beside it, he is then sure to be cured. This shrine was built in 1890. This fair provides occasion for folk songs and folk dances. Young people form themselves into groups and go about dancing and singing for hours. Some dancers don women's dress and perform Giddha for the sake of fun. The fair lasts for three days.

Jarag Fair

This fair is held in Jarag, a village in tehsil pail. It is held in Chet (March-April) in honour of the goddess Seetla. It is also known as the Baheria fair. Sweet gurgulas (jaggery cakes fried in oil) are prepared one day earlier and then given in offering to the goddess and thereafter to the donkey who is her favourite. After propitiating the goddess, the family members eat the remaining Savoury gurgulas with great relish. This festival is observed in Malwa and Powad, but the fair is held only in Jarag. There is a pond where the devotees of Seetla gather. They scoop the earth and raise a small hillock which is accorded the status of the goddess's shrine. Potters specially bring their donkeys decked in colored blankets. Some even put bells or conch shells and beads round their necks. In many folk songs of the Punjab, there is a reference to the fair of Jarag.

Roshni Fair

The Roshni (lights) Fair is held in Jagranvan from the 14th to the 16th of Phalgun in honour of the Muslim Pir, Abdul Kader Jalani. It is held in the vicinity of his tomb. Although it is a Muslim fair in origin, the Hindus of the area also flock to the site of this shrine. It is called the 'fair of lights' because innumerable devotees who come to visit the place light earthen lamps at the shrine of the Pir. The lights are visible from long distances. It is believed that whatever wish one sincerely makes, at the shrine of this Pir is granted. Young people sing Bolian and perform dances, thus adding to the gaiety and glamour of the fair. It is sheer delight to villagers performing dances and singing songs to the sweet strains of the flute and the one-stringed instrument called Toomba.

Some fairs are held at places associated with the lives of some Sikh Gurus, such as the Masya fair in Taran Taran, and the Muktsar fair in Ferozepur. Small fairs are periodically held here and there all over the Punjab. In Phalgun a fair in memory of Guru Nanak is held on the full-moon night at Dera Baba Nanak. At Jindwal (Navanshehar), a fair is held near a pond on Baisakhi day, at a spot where once Shri Guru Hargobind is believed to have sat. At Nanaksar in Hakeempur (Navanshehar), a fair is held at the place where the seventh Guru, Guru Harirai, stayed for some time.

Muktsar Fair

The Muktsar fair is one of the largest Sikh fairs held in Punjab. The fair is held in the middle of January on the Makar Sankranti day.

The festival is in commemoration of a battle fought in 1705-1706 by Guru Gobind Singh against the pursuing imperial forces which overtook him here and cut his followers to pieces. The Guru himself escaped and had the bodies of his followers disposed of with the usual rites. He declared that they had all obtained mukti and promised the same blessing to all his followers, who should thereafter, on the anniversary of that day, bathe in the Holy pool which had been filled by rain from heaven in answer to his prayer for water. On this spot a fine tank was afterwards dug by Maharaja Ranjit Singh and called Muktsar (the pool of Salvation).

It is one of the great Sikh festivals, and lasts three days. On the first day the worshippers bathe is the sacred tank. On the second day the people go in a procession (mohalla) to the three holy mounds which lie to the north-west of the town, namely, Rikab Sahib, Tibbi Sahib and Mukhwanjana Sahib. The Rikab Sahib, a mound formed out of the handfuls of earth taken from the tank by the faithful and thrown there, commemorates the spot where the Guru's stirrup broke.

The procession goes up the slope to the Tibbi Sahib which, crowned with a Gurudwara, is the mound where Guru Gobind Singh stood and aimed his arrows at the imperial forces. The devotes then proceed to the Mukhwanjana Sahib where the Guru is said to have cleaned his teeth with a tooth-stick. Prayers are offered here and the devotes then return. This mound has been built in the same way as the Rikab Sahib. On their return trip people visit the Tambu Sahib where the Guru's tent was pitched before the fight started, the Shahid Ganj, which is the Samadhi of the forty martyrs and the Darbar Sahib, where the Guru held his Darbar after the cremation of the slain.

OTHER FAIRS

Another big fair is held for four days every year in Malerkotla at the shrine of Haider Sheikh. It is largely attended. It is believed that if childless women visit the shrine and offers rots (large sweet cakes) specially cooked, they will be blessed with child.

There are various other small fairs which are similarly held in memory of Saints and Sages. On the 14th of Chet, a fair is held in Dhesian Sang (Philaur) at the shrine and in honour of Baba Sang. Another fair is held at the tomb of Khwaja Roshan in Har on every first Thursday after the new moon. In Nakodar, a Hindu-Muslim fair is held at village Kara at the shrine of Mir Shah Husain, who, according to legend, lived about five hundred years ago. At Khatkar Kalan (Navanshehar), a fair is held on Baisakhi day in memory of Baba Jawahar Singh. Another fair, Shiv Chaudas, is held at Paddi Matwali (Navanshehar) on the 14th of Chet on the bank of the river Bein.

In March, at Nathana (Ferozepur) a fair is held in honour of a Hindu Saint, Kalu. He is said to have dug a large pond in one scoop and deposited the dug-up earth in a closely heap which now forms the object of popular veneration.

Festivals constitute a special feature in the cultural life of the Punjabi's. There is seldom a month without a festival. Small festivals are numerous.

The festivals connected with the lunar days such as Ekadashi (eleventh lunar day), Poornamashi (full moon), and Masya (new moon) occur every month. Similarly, Sankranti, when the sun enters the new Zodiac sign, is celebrated on the first of every month of the Vikrami era with great gusto. It is also an occasion to prepare and eat the nicest of foods.

On festival days people get up early in the morning and have a bath, because religious traditions attach great ceremonial importance to bathing. Water is regarded as a purifying agent, and a clean body, it is believed, harbours and nourishes a pure soul. Women don their best dresses and wear jewellery. It is also an occasion when a lot of fuss is made about sending gifts to the daughters of the family.

In the Punjab, where the Vikrami era is followed, the year begins with Chet (March-April). On the first of this month the arrival of the new year is celebrated by the performance of a ritual of taking the new corn, known as Ann Nawan Karna. Sheaf's of new Corn are roasted and then the parched grain is eaten. Everyone must have a bath on the new year day, and put on new clothes. Delicacies like kheer and halwa are prepared and eaten.

The Sankranti of Baisakh, the second month of the year, is an important day, and is celebrated in much the same way, only with an added accent on eating, drinking and merry-making, which are counter-balanced by charity and fasting. Baiskakhi is one of the most popular festivals of the Punjab with fairs held at various places.

On the eleventh day of the bright half of Jeth (May-June) falls Nirjala Ekadashi, which is better known in the Punjab as Nimani Kasti. Hindus, especially women observe fast on this day and smear the body with powdered sandal wood. This fast is very hard to keep because for the whole day one has to abstain even from water. Charitably inclined people put up stalls for free distribution of sweetened and chilled water. The stalls known as chhabils, are a common sight on this day.

Teeyan, a festival of the rainy season, is celebrated on the 3rd of the bright fortnight of Sawan (July-August). The four months from Harh (June-July) to the first half of Assu (September) are called Chaumasa. During this period the sky generally remains overcast and the weather shifts between sultriness and rainfall. Rains bring the longed-for relief to the heat-stricken Punjabis, and the rhythm of the little and big drops of rain instills in them the enthusiasm which must seek expression in fun and frolic. A newly-married girl looks forward to the rainy days when a brother or some other male relative from the parental home may come to escort her to her father's place.

This reversal from bride hood to being just a daughter again is such a liberating and thrilling experience that it cannot be put into words. One day before the Teeyan, girls apply henna to their hands and feet, and on the day of the festival they put on their best clothes and go out to the fair. The fair resounds with the songs of love and the rhythm of dance. The songs are known as Teeyan songs. The Giddha dance has become a regular and most enchanting feature of this festival. At home women make kheer, a dish specially associated with Sawan.

In Bhadon, on the day of the full moon, the Rakhi festival is celebrated. On this day sisters tie the multi-coloured thread on the right wrist of their brothers. So long as a sister has not tied the Rakhi to her brother, she is not supposed to eat anything. After she has done so she offers some sweets to her brother and he in return gives her some gift or money. Rakhi is meant to remained the brother of his promise to protect his sister whenever she needs this protection.

Gugga Naumi, which is a festival in honour of Gugga Pir, also falls in Bhadon. The Pir's devotees paint his image on the wall in turmeric, as also paint a snake in black, right in front of it and then perform the ritual of worship. People also pour butter milk into the holes of snakes. Sweet Sevian is the special dish of the festival. The Halbagis, who are devout followers of Gugga Pir, also known as Zahir Pir, erect a long pole covered with flags, coloured cloth, coconuts, etc. and render worship to it as to a god. The devotees carry the Pir's stand from house and beg. The disciple who carries the standard is known as the Pir's house. To propitiate Gugga Pir women sing songs in his admiration.

The fifteen lunar days of the dark half of the moon in Assu are the Shradh days when the dead are propitiated. People observe this rite out of moral obligation and gratitude to the manes. Brahmins are fed on the particular ancestor died. During these days nothing auspicious is celebrated. The Shradhs are followed by the Nauratas (Navaratras), which regarded auspicious for celebration on the first of the mix days barley is sown in the house. This is called Khetri, or goddess Gorjas farm. This little farm is watered and nurtured regularly till the eighth or ninth day. On that day goddess Gorja, in the form of seedlings, is covered with a piece of red cloth and worshipped and propitiated. Hindu women observe a fast during the Nauratas, though esculent roots like potates, and cakes made from the water-chestnut (sandhara) flour are allowed despite the fast. On the Dussehra day women cut the young shoots of Khetri and tick them in the headwears of their male relatives, and invariably get gifts in return. The festival of goddess Sanjhi is also celebrated during the Nauratas. On the first day an image of the goddess is made from mixing mud and cow dung and is then placed along a wall on a door. Every evening during the Nauratas the image is worshipped, incantations are muttered and an offering of a mixture of rice and sugar (tilcholi) is distributed. On the day of Dussehra this image is immersed in water.

The Dussehra festival is celebrated in a big way. Big tall effigies of Ravana, Kumbkharna and Meghnad are burnt at a large number of places. During the Nauratas Ram-Lila is organised at innumerable places in the state. On Kartik on the fourth day falls Karva Chauth. On this day married women observe a fast and pray for the long life of their husbands. Sometimes unmarried girls observe this fast and pray for their husbands-to-be. This is the mother-in-laws day because it is customary on this day for the daughter-in-law to present her offerings (Baya) in the form of money and eatables. On the eleventh lunar day in this month the festival of Devuthan (waking up the deities) is celebrated. Metal plates are taken in order to awaken the deities who are supposed to go to sleep between the summer harvest and the first ploughing after the start of the autumnal rains.

The most important festival in the month of Kartik is Diwali. Eearthen lamps or candles are lighted over buildings all over the state. People celebrate the festival with great gusto. Houses are white-washed, new clothes are purchased and sweets of all kinds are prepared. People worship Goddess Lakshmi with an offering of sweets and silver coins. Thereafter they distribute sweets among friends and relatives. It is believed that on this night Goddess Lakshmi in the company of Vidmata (goddess of fate) takes a round of every and wherever she takes a fancy, she bestows immense prosperity. In the Golden Temple of Amristar, Diwali is celebrated with great eclat. Earthen lamps are lighted all round the hold tank and their undulating refelctions in the water look extremely fascinating.

14th January Lohri which comes on is another popular festival of Punjab. A few days before it arrives, youngsters get together in groups and go round their localities singing folk-songs connected with Lohri and collecting fuel and money for the bonfire. This is a special day for making offerings to fire. When fire is lit up in the evening, orthodox men and women go round it, pour offerings into it and bow before it in reverence. The first Lohri for a new bride or a new-born baby is celebrated enthusiastically and sweets are distributed.

Next day after Lohri comes Maghi. It is a popular festival of the Punjabis. On this day fairs are held at many places, people go out for a holy dip and give away a lot in charity. The special dish of the day is kheer cooked in sugarcane juice. The most colourful and hilarious of all the festivals which are celebrated in the Punjab is Holi which is celebrated on the full-moon day of Phagun. A big fair known as Hola Mahala is held at Anandpur on the next day after Holi. Villagers come from far-off places to join it. Some festivals are held in the Punjab in honour of the Sikh Gurus. These are called Gurupureabs.

They are well spread over the year. There are three important Gurupurabs. On the full moon of Karthik the birth anniversary of Guru Nanak is celebrated by the devotees with great ardour. Two days earlier a non-stop reading of the Adi Granth is started. At different places religious congregations are held and hymns from the Granth Sahib are chanted. Large processions are taken out through the towns. At night buildings are illuminated. The birth anniversary of Guru Gobind Singh is also celebrated in a similar manner. The third important Gurupurab is the one associated with the martyrdom of Guru Arjun Dev.

10

Education

INTRODUCTION

Primary and Secondary education is mainly affiliated to Punjab School Education Board. Punjab is served by several institutions of higher education, including 23 universities that provide undergraduate and postgraduate courses in all the major arts, humanities, science, engineering, law, medicine, veterinary science, and business. Punjab Agricultural University is a leading institution globally for the study of agriculture and played a significant role in Punjab's Green Revolution in the 1960s–70s. Alumni of the Panjab University, Chandigarh include Manmohan Singh, the former Prime Minister of India, and Dr. Har Gobind Khorana, a biochemistry nobel laureate.

The National Institute of Pharmaceutical Education and Research

The Ranjit Singh Block at Guru Nanak Dev University

Guru Gobind Singh Bhawan at Punjabi University

One of the oldest institutions of medical education is the Christian Medical College, Ludhiana, which has existed since 1894. There is an existing gap in education between men and women, particularly in rural areas of Punjab. Of a total of 1 million 300 thousand students enrolled in grades five to eight, only 44% are women.

Punjab has 23 universities, of which 10 are private, 9 are state, 1 is central and 3 are deemed universities. Punjab has 1.04 lakh (104,000) engineering seats.

Punjab also putting step in education of Yoga and Naturopathy. It's slowly becoming popular and student adopting these as their career . Board of Naturopathy and yoga science (B.N.Y.S.) Regional College Dinanagar is very first college opened in Dinanagar Town with the help of Dr Jawahar lal Raina and Dr Abhishek Gaur.

PRIMARY AND SECONDARY EDUCATION

The Indian government lays emphasis on the primary education up to the age of fourteen years, referred to as elementary education in India. The Indian government has also banned child labour in order to ensure that the children do not enter unsafe working conditions. However, both free education and the ban on child labour are difficult to enforce due to economic disparity and social conditions. 80% of all recognized schools at the elementary stage are government run or supported, making it the largest provider of education in the country.

School workshop

However, due to a shortage of resources and lack of political will, this system suffers from massive gaps including high pupil to teacher ratios, shortage of infrastructure and poor levels of teacher training. Figures released by the Indian government in 2011 show that there were 5,816,673 elementary school teachers in India. As of March 2012 there were 2,127,000 secondary school teachers in India. Education has also been made free for children for 6 to 14 years of age or up to class

VIII under the Right of Children to Free and Compulsory Education Act 2009.

There have been several efforts to enhance quality made by the government. The District Education Revitalization Programme (DERP) was launched in 1994 with an aim to universalize primary education in India by reforming and vitalizing the existing primary education system.85% of the DERP was funded by the central government and the remaining 15 percent was funded by the states. The DERP, which had opened 160000 new schools including 84000 alternative education schools delivering alternative education to approximately 3.5 million children, was also supported by UNICEF and other international programmes.

This primary education scheme has also shown a high Gross Enrollment Ratio of 93–95% for the last three years in some states.Significant improvement in staffing and enrollment of girls has also been made as a part of this scheme. The current scheme for universalization of Education for All is the Sarva Shiksha Abhiyan which is one of the largest education initiatives in the world. Enrollment has been enhanced, but the levels of quality remain low.

Secondary Education

The National Policy on Education (NPE), 1986, has provided for environment awareness, science and technology education, and introduction of traditional elements such as Yoga into the Indian secondary school system. Secondary education covers children aged 14 to 18, 88.5 million children according to the Census, 2001.

A significant feature of India's secondary school system is the emphasis on inclusion of the disadvantaged sections of the society. Professionals from established institutes are often called to support in vocational training. Another feature of India's secondary school system is its emphasis on profession based vocational training to help students attain skills for finding a vocation of his/her choosing. A significant new feature has been the extension of SSA to secondary education in the form of the Rashtriya Madhyamik Shiksha Abhiyan.

A special Integrated Education for Disabled Children (IEDC) programme was started in 1974 with a focus on primary education. but which was converted into Inclusive Education at Secondary Stage Another notable special programme, the *Kendriya Vidyalaya* project, was started for the employees of the central government of India, who are distributed throughout the country. The government started the *Kendriya Vidyalaya* project in 1965 to provide uniform education in institutions following the same syllabus at the same pace regardless of the location to which the employee's family has been transferred.

Classroom in Punjab

Tertiary education

Punjab is served by many public institutes of higher education (listed below). All the major arts, humanities, science, engineering, law, medicine, veterinary science, and business courses are offered, leading to first degrees as well as postgraduate awards. Advanced research is conducted in all major areas of excellence. Punjab Agricultural University is one of the world's leading authorities in agriculture. It was instrumental and played vital role in Punjab's Green Revolution in the 1960s-70s.

Universities

Central

- Central University of Punjab, Bathinda

State

- Panjab University, Chandigarh (a Punjab State University)
- Baba Farid University of Health Sciences, Faridkot
- Guru Nanak Dev University, Amritsar
- Punjab Agricultural University, Ludhiana
- IK Gujral Punjab Technical University, Jalandhar
- Maharaja Ranjit Singh Punjab Technical University, Bathinda
- Punjabi University, Patiala
- Guru Ravidas Ayurved University, Hoshiarpur
- Guru Angad Dev Veterinary and Animal Sciences University, Ludhiana
- Rajiv Gandhi National University of Law, Patiala

Deemed

- Sant Longowal Institute of Engineering and Technology, Longowal(Deemed)
- Thapar University, Patiala(Deemed)

Private

- Apeejay Institute of Management Technical Campus, Jalandhar (Punjab)
- Sri Guru Granth Sahib World University, Fatehgarh Sahib
- GGS College of Modern Technology, Kharar
- Indian School of Business, Ajitgarh

- Guru Kashi University, Talwandi Sabo
- DAV University, Jalandhar

Thapar University

- GNA University, Phagwara
- Sant Baba Bhag Singh University, Jalandhar
- Akal University

Autonomous colleges in Punjab

Many colleges of Punjab have been granted autonomous status by UGC.

- Khalsa College, Amritsar
- Mata Gujri College, Fatehgarh Sahib
- S.G.G.S. Khalsa College, Mahilpur (Hoshiarpur district)
- Amritsar College of Engineering & Technology
- Beant College of Engineering and Technology Gurdaspur
- Shaheed Bhagat Singh State Technical Campus, Ferozepur
- Guru Nanak Dev Engineering College, Ludhiana

Reputed colleges (Technical /Professional)

- Apeejay Institute of Management Technical Campus, Jalandhar (Punjab)
- Desh Bhagat Group of Institutes, Gobindgarh, Moga, Muktsar under Desh Bhagat University
- Indian Institute of Technology, Ropar
- Indian Institute of Management Amritsar
- Indian Institute of Science Education and Research, Mohali
- Dr B R Ambedkar National Institute of Technology, Jalandhar
- Global Institute Of Management & Emerging Technologies, Amritsar
- Institute of Nano Science and Technology (INST), Mohali
- Giani Zail Singh Punjab Technical University Campus (Government Engineering College), Bathinda
- Malout institute of Management & Technology, Malout (Govt. of Punjab)
- Bhutta College of Engineering & Technology, Ludhiana
- Malwa College of Nursing
- Baba Banda Singh Bahadur Engineering college,Fatehgarh Sahib
- Sri Sukhmani Institute of Engineering & Technology, Dera Bassi(Mohali)

Other Institutes of Repute (General)

- Aryabhatta group of institutions, Barnala
- BBK DAV College for Women, Amritsar
- BCM College of Education, Ludhiana
- College of Engineering and Management, Kapurthala
- Desh Bhagat Group of Institutes, Gobindgarh, Moga, Muktsar under Desh Bhagat University
- [Doraha college of Education, Doraha]

- GHG Khalsa College of Education, GURUSAR Sudhar
- Govt. Bikram College of Commerce, Patiala
- Govt. College of Education, Sector 20 Chandigarh
- Govt. Barjinder College, Faridkot
- Desh Bhagat Pt. Chetan Dev Govt.College of Education, Faridkot
- Gulzar Group of Institutes, Khanna (Engineering College)
- Malwa Group of Institutions.
- Khalsa College, Patiala
- Kings Group of Institutions, Barnala,Punjab
- Malwa College of Nursing, Kotkapura
- Mohindra College, Patiala
- PCTE Group of Institutes (including Punjab College of Technical Education), Ludhiana
- Punjab Engineering College, Chandigarh
- Regional Centre Punjabi University, Bathinda
- SGGS Khalsa College Sector 26 Chandigarh
- State College of Education, Patiala
- Swami Sarvanand Giri Panjab University Regional Centre, Hoshiarpur

Medical Colleges

As of 2015, there are more than 920 MBBS and 1,070 BDS seats across Punjab.

Government Medical Colleges

- Government Medical College, Amritsar
- Guru Gobind Singh Medical College, Faridkot
- Government Medical College, Patiala

Private Medical Colleges

- Gian Sagar Medical College & Hospital, Patiala
- Sri Guru Ram Das Institute of Medical Sciences & Research, Sri Amritsar

- Punjab Institute of Medical Sciences, Jalandhar
- Christian Medical College, Ludhiana
- Dayanand Medical College & Hospital, Ludhiana
- Adesh Institute of Medical Sciences & Research, Bathinda
- Chintpurni Medical College, Gurdaspur
- Desh Bhagat School of Medical Sciences, Mandi Gobindgarh Desh Bhagat University.

PUNJAB SCHOOL EDUCATION BOARD

Power Functions

Academic Wing

Examination Wing

Administration Wing

The Punjab School Education Board came into being under an Act of Legislation in 1969, amended in 1987, 2000 and 2005.

Power functions:

(1) Subject to the provisions of this Act, the Board shall exercise and perform the following powers namely:

(i) prescribe the syllabi, courses of the studies and text books for school education;

(ii) organize research for grading of textual vocabulary and arrange for regular revision of text books and other books;

(iii) hold examinations for school education, publish the results of such examinations and grant certificates to the persons, who have passed such examinations;

(iv) admit to the examinations, on the prescribed conditions, candidates, who have pursued the prescribed courses of instructions, whether in affiliated institutions or otherwise. However; any change in the prevalent conditions shall be made with the prior approval of the State Government;

(v) cause enquiries to be made through such agency and in such manner, as may be prescribed regarding the conditions prevailing in an institution before it is admitted to the privileges of the Board and require such agency to inspect affiliated institutions and submit a report to the Board as to how for the conditions privileges of the Board, are being compiled with;

(vi) prescribe penalties for misconduct pertaining to examinees, examiners and other persons engaged in the conduct of examinations;

(vii) appoint examiners and supervisory staff and fix their enumeration;

(viii) lay down conditions and restrictions for admission of candidates to the examination;

(ix) organize and provide lectures, demonstration, educational tours, exhibitions, seminars and symposia and take such other measures, as may be necessary to raise and promote the quality and standard of school teaching and education;

(x) submit annual audited accounts and balance sheets together with the report of the Board to the State Government not later than the 30th September of the next year and publish such accounts and balance sheets in the official Gazette;

(xi) give grants to the State Council of Educational Research and Training for educational activities and research work;

(xii) institute and award scholarships, medals and prizes;

(xiii) fix, demand and receive such fees and other charges, as may be prescribed;

(xiv) hold any property and receive bequests, donations, endowments, trusts and transfer of any property or interest therein or right thereto;

(xv) prescribe measures for the intellectual, physical, moral and ethical promotion and for social welfare of students in affiliated institutions and the conditions of their residence and discipline

(xvi) encourage sports and health-building activities;

(xvii) take measures for the welfare of teachers of affiliated institutions and employees of the Board;

(xviii) do such other acts and things, as it may deem fit for the purpose of carrying out the provisions of this Act.

(2) Subject to the provisions of this Act, the Board shall exercise and perform the following powers and functions with prior approval of the State Government, namely:

(a) arrange for the preparation, writing, compilation, printing, publishing and sale of text books, other educational material and undertake the publication of any other educational work, book or periodicals. However, copy right of any material developed, published, printed by the Board, shall vest with the state Government; and

(b) prescribe conditions for affiliation of institution in terms of teachers and their qualification, curriculum, equipments, buildings and other education: facilities'.

Term of office of chairman, vice-Chairman and members:

(1) The term of office of the Chairman and Vice-Chairman shall be three years from the date of publication of the notification under sub section (4) of 4, which may further be extended for a period of two years: Provided that no person appointed as Chairman of Vice-Chairman shall continue as such beyond the age of sixty-two years.

(2) The term of office of a nominated member shall be two years from the date of his nomination, which may further be extended for a period of two years.

"Not with standing anything contained in sub-section (1), the term of office of an officer of the State Government, sent on deputation, as Chairman or Vice-Chairman shall be such, as may be fixed by the State Government, but it shall in no case, exceed three years".

Term of Office of Secretary

The Board shall appoint a person to be its Secretary from a panel prepared and sent by the State Government consisting of the officers of the State Government and the eligible officers of Board for a term of three years, which may further be extended by the Board for a period of two years. If a person is appointed as Secretary from amongst the officers of the State Government, his appointment as such, shall be treated on deputation and it shall be governed by the relevant rules or policy instructions of the Punjab Government shall be governed by the relevant rules or policy instructions of the Punjab Government.

Provided that no person appointed as Secretary of the Board shall continue as such beyond the age of superannuation prescribed for the employees of the Board".

Academic Wing

This wing comprises of four major branches *i.e.* Academic Branch, Open School, Punjabi Cell and Field Programme which are being supervised by four Deputy Directors who in turn are assisted by Subject Experts and Project Officers. The academic wing is headed by the Director Academics. Besides preparing the syllabi and text-books for the school classes, this wing organises educational competitions for the school children. The Open School Branch caters to the educational needs of the out of school children of the state. To provide quality education to the rural children, 9 Adarsh Schools run by the Board, are also being looked after by this wing. Board spends Rs. 4 crore annually to run these schools. One of the responsibilities of this wing is to keep a liaison with the NCERT, New Delhi, SCERT and other sister organisations involved in similar educational activities at the National/ State levels to make periodical changes and update the text-books as per the latest thinking on different educational issues.

Publication of Text Books

This wing is headed by Deputy Director and assisted by the publication Officers, Assistant publication Officers and other supporting staff. The responsibility of this wing is to engage the private printing presses to get the text-books printed. At present, there are 210 titles apart from the other publications like syllabi, guidebooks.

Sale of Text Books

The Board has established text-books sale depots at District and some Tehsil levels. At present there are 21 text-books sale depots.

This wing is headed by a Deputy Secretary who is assisted by Senior Managers at head office and managers at district level/ tehsil levels. The depots are dealing with the sale of textbooks, admission forms and syllabi for different classes. There are 2504 sale agencies which procure the books, admission forms and syllabi from the depots on commission basis.

Examination Wing

This wing is headed by the Controller of Examinations assisted by Deputy Secretaries and Assistant Secretaries. The responsibility of this wing is to conduct the Matriculation and +2 examinations, to get evaluate the answer-books and to declare results and to issue certificates etc.. This wing supervise about 4000 examination centres all over the state.

To ensure copying free conduct of examinations different flying squads headed by D.E.O. and other officers of Board and Education Department are deputed to check the copying. To stop the outside interference help of police is sought and section 144 of Cr. P. C. is also activated.

Middle Cell

This wing is headed by the Deputy Secretary assisted by Assistant Secretaries and Superintendents. The responsibility of this wing is to conduct the Middle standard examination, to get evaluate the answer-books and to declare results and to issue certificates etc..

Administrative Wing

This wing is headed by the Secretary assisted by the Finance & Development Officer, Joint Secretary, Deputy Secretaries, Assistant Secretaries etc. This wing deals with the Establishment and Administration. The responsibility of the

Finance & Development Officer is to maintain accounts of the Board and their profitable investments and to prepare budget.

The financial position for the year 2005-2006 is as under:

Income	8226.58 lacs
Expenditure	8605.39 lacs
Loss	378.81 lacs

The Board also gives merit scholarships to meritorious students @ one student per 1000 students. These scholarships are given only to those students who are not covered by the national/state scholarships. At present there are 1739 Schools affiliated to the Punjab School Education Board.

State Council of Education Research & Training: Established in 1981, the various units of SCERT lay the main thrust on the Pre-service and In-service teacher training, as envisaged in the National Policy of Education.

For discharging the duty of Pre-service to the teachers, 13 District Institutes of Education and training are there in existence and JBT school are imparting Pre-service training to the primary teachers. For giving In-service training to the already working secondary teachers, 12 In-service Training Centres are functioning at District Headquarters in the State.

In Addition State Institute of Science Education imparts In-service training to Science Teachers/Math Teachers. To impart training in the latest advance educational technology, SCERT organizes seminars for teachers through educational technology Cell.

To bring quantitative improvement in education SCERT keeps the latest comparative data through Data Processing Unit. Qualitative aspect of Education being the main objective of SCERT the Evaluation Unit achieve this purpose by working on the Examination Reforms. Educational and Vocational Guidance Bureau motivates the students and teachers towards the dignity of labour and self-employment to save the future generation from frustration resulting out of un-employment because of over population.

Objectives

To bring about qualitative improvement in the existing educational system of the State;

To develop syllabi and curricula of the various subjects at School stage:

To undertake and promote investigations, surveys, studies and researches in various fields/sectors of education;

To provide Pre and In-service education for teachers and educational supervisors.

To formulate and implement pilot projects for bringing about qualitative improvement in different fields of school education;

To develop new techniques and methodologies in the field of school education;

To monitor and develop educational programmes;

To introduce and implements New Education Policies Centre/State.

Defined objectives of the wings of SCERT are achieved through its different units.

Survey and Data Processing Unit

Survey and Data Processing Unit acts as Data Bank for SCERT.

It collects and processes data relating to various facets of school education, evolves application of sample surveys and techniques, collects theme oriented studies and prepares long range series of data on various facets of education and undertakes projections.

Educational Technology Cell & Film Library

The Educational Technology Cell aims at improving the standard of education at all levels. In collaboration with All India Radio Workshops are organized to identify the talent potential and prepare good radio lessons. Motivational material is prepared to help achieve the Universalisation of elementary education. The importance of imparting education through mass media, *e.g.*, Radio, TV. Films and Printed Material, is emphasized to make education more functional and relevant.

Organisation of Training Courses in Audio-Visual Education.

Organisation of Film Library including loaning of Films & other Components to schools.

Inspection and Repair of Audio-Visual Education Machinery of the Schools/Institutions.

Devising and making experiments and popularizing new Audio Visual Aids/Techniques.

Collection of Central Audio-Visual fund from the Schools at the State Headquarters and keeps its account.

To make improvement in the Audio-Visual Education in the State Schools.

To assist for the purchase of Audio-Visual Education material.

Pre-view of Children Films.

Misc. work regarding Audio-Visual Education.

Modern Technology -Audio- Visual Education

Necessary programme for the TV Cassettes /Video Cassettes and its duplication is being done so that students while studying in the schools may get necessary knowledge/guidance in the present Technical-era according the New Education Policy.

STATE EVALUATION UNIT

Special Orientation of Primary Teachers (SOPT)

Under the Centrally sponsored scheme of Special Orientation of Primary School Teachers. The main aim of SOPT training is to orient the Primary School teachers to the teaching methodology with special reference to competency based teaching *i.e.* Minimum levels of learning, child centred approach of education, operation black board and comprehensive and continuos evaluation.

Implementation of MLL Scheme

The scheme of MLL was introduced in a phased manner in this State through DIETs. To bring with it was introduced in only two blocks of Distt. Patiala, *i.e.*, Bhadson I & II. At present it has been implemented in all the schools of Distt. Ludhiana from class I to V. In other districts, the scheme is being implemented in the lab areas attached to functional DIETs. The teachers/educators are also being trained simultaneously to make it more effective. Sample question papers are also prepared by the DIET faculties to test the child's achievements, *i.e.*, desired competencies literature has been/being prepared/translated.

State Institute of Science Education

In-service Training Courses are arranged for science and maths teachers in updating their knowledge about changes, innovation and new curriculum developments in the subject of science and mathematics. Science Institute organised Science exhibition/Student seminars at Teshil/Distt/State level under National Talent Search Examination (NTSE) Scheme brilliant students at class X level are identified State wise by a preliminary screening test. Population education Project is funded by UNFPA and Punjab Govt. Main aim of this project is to develop the concept of small family norms.

State Bureau of Education and Vocational Guidance

The State Bureau of Educational and Vocational Guidance disseminates career information to the students particularly at the terminal stages and thereby directs towards self-employment to save them from the formidable problems of unemployment due to population explosion. To help them take care in keeping with their aptitudes, tastes and mental levels.

Technical Education

The Department of Technical Education & Industrial Training was created on 10.06.77 in its present form after detaching the

Technical Education Wing from the Department of Punjab, PWD (B&R) and detaching the Industrial Training Wing out of the Department of industries thereby bringing both the wings under one umbrella though each of these two Wings are more than 50 years old.

The Department has two Wings. The Technical Education Wing of Department of Technical Education and Industrial Training has been entrusted with the responsibility of managing Degree and Diploma level Institutions in the State of Punjab. The Department is looking after the management and pharmacy institutions. The work in the Department is mostly governed by the norms, guidelines and regulations of All India Council for Technical Education which has been established under Central Act. The Department also looks after the work relating to Punjab Technical University, Jalandhar and Engineering Colleges fully funded or partially funded by the Government.

To meet the global competition, seats are being increased in Information Technology and related courses at 21 Degree Level Engineering Colleges. Similarly, the Diploma Course in Information Technology is being introduced in 15 Polytechnic Institutes.

Facility of Internet Connectivity is provided through AICTE ERNet Scheme, under this all Engineering Colleges and Diploma Level Institutes are provided leased line connections. E-Commerce course has been introduced by Punjab Technical University in 4 Technical Institutions for employability to the youth of Punjab.

Smart Card System is introduced in all Engineering Colleges and Diploma Level Institutes.

The Industrial Training Wing of Department of Technical Education and Industrial Training has been entrusted with the responsibility of imparting training in Engineering and non-engineering trades to cater the need of the industry in respect of skilled workers. All the Industrial Training Institutes work under Craftsman Training Scheme of Government of India, Director-General Employment & Training under the directions of National Council of Vocational Training which the apex body at Government of India level for coordinating development of Industrial Training in the country. Similar to the National Council for Vocational Training at Central level, State Council for Vocational Training the State level is responsible for coordinating an integrated development of Industrial Training.

Ten Institute Management Committees (IMCs) have been set up for ITI's to involve the concerned Industry in the day-to-day management of the Institutions. This will also ensure acceptability of the final product by the Industry.

Hi-Tech Training Institute established under Vocational Training Project had started functioning. Training in four Hi-Tech courses of Auto CAD, PC Maintenance, Industrial Automation and Analogue and Digital Electronics is being provided to Industrial in service personnel.

Similarly, special attention is being paid to the Punjab Technical University and it is proposed to make this University as a centre of excellence. Post Graduate and Post Doctoral subjects in emerging branches in technology are being planned to be started from the new financial year.

To further improve the quality of training for catering to the changing needs of the Industry 362 Memoranda of Understanding on Technical Education side and Memoranda of Understanding on Industrial Training side have been signed with industry so as to enable the human resources of these Technical Institutions acceptable to the Industry.

For attaining these objectives, approved plan provision for 10th Five Year Plan is Rs. 66.88 crores for Technical Education Wing. The Government for 2003-2004 has approved plan Budget for Rs. 4.87 crores for Technical Education Wing.

The Department is looking after 41 Engineering Colleges, 15 B. Pharmacy colleges, 46 MBA, MCA, BBA, BCA private unaided Institutions and 46 Polytechnics & Pharmacy institutions and more than 172 Industrial Training Institutes including the ones in the private sector. Every year a total of about 17640 Engineers, 7215 Diploma holders and about 24,474 other technical manpower at Industrial Training Institute level.

During the 2002-2003 year, 443 Engineering, 1269 Polytechnics and 1707 ITIs students have been placed in the various Industrial Units. The Technical Education wing has a total staff strength of 689 Class A, 18 Class B, 626 Class C and 376 Class D in the Polytechnics and 16 Class A, 3 Class B, 73 Class C and 24 Class D in Directorate.

Industrial training wing has a total staff strength of 54 Class A, 252 class B, 2131 Class C, 1092 Class D in the ITIs and 21 Class A, 11 class B, 121 Class C, 35 Class D in the Directorate.

A Technical Education System should not only be responsible to the new innovations in technologies, but it should also be in tune with the contemporary industrial culture and economic environments. To alleviate the feelings of the industry that the existing Technical Education System was not keeping pace with the technological advances in the related fields, the Government of Punjab has taken a number of steps for toning up the technical education systems at all levels.

The Department of Technical Education and Industrial Training is committed to bring about quality improvement, modernization and capacity expansion in the Technical Education System to fulfill the aspirations and expectations of the industry in today's globally competitive new industrial and economic environments driven by the advanced and emerging technologies. This will also ensure better job opportunities and brighter future for the youngsters and at the same time help in achieving high productivity for the industry for facing the challenges of a new liberalized economy.

Bibliography

Avtar Singh: *Ethics of the Sikhs*. Patiala 1970

Banerjee, Indubhusan: *Evolution of the Khalsa*. Calcutta: A. Mukerjee, 1963.

Bhagat Lakshman: *Short Sketch of the Life and Works of Guru Gobind Singh*. Asian Educational Services.

Cole, William: *The Sikhs: Their Religious Beliefs and Practice*. Sussex Academic Press, 1995.

Cunningham, J.D.: *A History of the Sikhs,* Delhi, 1966.

Davey Cunningham: *A History Of The Sikhs*. John Murray,London, 1853.

Gerald, N. : *The Sikhs and Their Literature,* Delhi, 1970.

Harbans Singh: *Berkeley Lectures on Sikhism*, Manohar Publication, Delhi, 1995.

Jasbir Kaur Ahuja: *The Zafarnama of Guru Gobind Singh*. Mumbai: Bharatiya Vidya Bhavan. 1996.

Jasbir Singh Ahluwalia: *The Doctrine and Dynamics of Sikhism*, Punjabi University, 2001.

John Clark: *The Sikhs,* Princeton, Delhi, 1946.

Kapur, A, Rajiv: *Sikh Separatism : The Politics of Faith,* London, 1986.

Kartar Singh Bhalla: *Let's Know Sikhism : A Religion of Harmony, Brotherhood and Tolerance*, Star Publication, Delhi, 2002.

Koenraad Elst: *Who is a Hindu? : Hindu Revivalist Views of Animism, Buddhism, Sikhism and Other Offshoots of Hinduism*, Voice of India, 2002.

Mahajan, V. D.: *Muslim Rule In India*. S. Chand, New Delhi, 1970.

Mahinder N Gulati: *Worlds Youngest Religion Sikhism : Islamic Influence and Tibetan Connection*, Atlantic Publication, 2007.

Mani Singh, Bhai: *Sikhan di Bhagat Mala*. Amritsar, 1955

McLeod, W.H; *The Sikhs : History, Religion and Society,* New York, 1989.

Nesbitt, Eleanor: *Sikhism: A Very Short Introduction*, Oxford University Press, USA, 2005.

Nikky Guninder and Kaur Singh: *Sikhism: An Introduction*, Viva Books, 2012.

Nirbani Singh: *Sikhism : Continuity of Indian Culture*, Kalpaz Publications, 2013.

Paramjit Singh: *501 Magnificent Facts About Sikhism*, Abhishek Publications, Delhi, 2011.

Pashaura Singh and N. Gerald Barrier: *Sikhism and History*, Oxford University Press, 2004.

Pashaura Singh: *Sikhism in Global Context*, Oxford University Press, 2011.

Prithi Pal: *The History of Sikh Gurus*. Lotus Books, 2007.

Richard, G. : *Lions of the Punjab : Culture in the Making,* New Delhi, 1987.

Sambhi, Piara Singh: *The Sikhs: Their Religious Beliefs and Practices.* London: Routledge & Kegan Paul. 1978.

Sandeep Goswami: *The Great Glory Sikhism*, Rupa Publication, 2006.

Satbir Singh: *Guru Tegh Bahadur; Commemorative Volume.* Publisher: Sri Guru Tegh Bahadur Tercentenary Martyrdom Gurpurab Committee. Govt. of India.1975

Singh, Bhai: *Sri Gur Pratap Suraj Granth.* Amritsar, 1927-35

Singh, Khushwant: *A History of the Sikhs: 1469-1839,* Oxford University Press, 1963.

Singh, Man : *Guru Gobind Singh: a literary survey.* New Delhi: Anmol Publications. 1989.

Singh, Pritam: *Federalism, Nationalism and Development: India and the Punjab Economy*, Routledge, 2008.

Singh, Sewa : *Sikhism (Religions of the World)*, Chelsea House Publications, 2005.

Singh, Surinder : *Guru Tegh Bahadur*, University of Wisconsin—Madison Center for South Asian Studies, 1975.

Sonali Bhatt Marwaha: *Colors of Truth : Religion, Self and Emotions : Perspectives of Hinduism, Buddhism, Jainism, Zoroastrianism, Islam, Sikhism and Contemporary Psychology*, Concept Publication, Delhi, 2006.

Teece, Geoff: *Sikhism: Religion in Focus*, Black Rabbit Books, 2004.

Index

M

P

R

S

T

V

W

❑❑❑